THE TAXPAYER'S

INTERNAL REVENUE SERVICE

AUDIT

SURVIVAL MANUAL

By Vernon K. Jacobs, C.P.A.
& Charles W. Schoeneman, Esq.

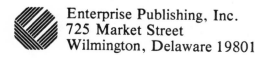

Enterprise Publishing, Inc.
725 Market Street
Wilmington, Delaware 19801

ISBN: 0-913864-70-6

Library of Congress Catalog No. 81-70892

Original Copyright 1980, Alexandria House Books

Copyright 1982 by Enterprise Publishing, Inc. Special Edition published by arrangement with Alexandria House books.

1st Printing, January 1982
2nd Printing, April 1982

Published by: Enterprise Publishing, Inc.
                 725 Market Street
                 Wilmington, Delaware 19801

Table of Contents

Chapter 4. Limited Contact Audits

Chapter 5: IRS Preliminaries

Chapter 6: The Taxpayer's Preparation

Chapter 7: The Audit Itself

Chapter 8: Closing an Audit

Chapter 9: Criminal Audits

Chapter 10: Collecting the Money

Chapter 11: Appeal within the IRS

Chapter 12: To the Courts

Chapter 13: Avoiding an Audit

Chapter 14: Closing Thoughts

Appendix 1: List of Unallowable Items

Preface

Chances are, the ongoing "battle" between tax collectors and taxpayers is the longest conflict in the history of man. When citizens believe that the taxes imposed by their government are reasonable and equitably distributed, the conflict subsides to a few isolated skirmishes. Under these conditions, most citizens would voluntarily pay what they regard as their fair share of the necessary costs of government. If tax collectors are perceived as servants of the public doing their job fairly, and the level of taxes is tolerable, taxpayers do not feel compelled to prepare for a war of wits with the tax authorities. And such a manual as you now have in your hands would be unnecessary.

But these peaceful conditions do not now exist in the United States. Most U.S. citizens believe the cost of government is no longer reasonable and that the tax load is unfairly distributed. While the citizenry disagrees on what government programs are necessary or unnecessary, most taxpayers recognize that the total cost of government is excessive and is destroying the American system. And they resent being compelled to pay for what they consider a wasteful and inefficient bureaucracy.

And, finally, we have reached the point where the tax collector has begun to act as master rather than servant of the public. In recent years, the Internal Revenue Service has started to play an active role in deciding what the rules should be. By administrative fiat, they have so rewritten the tax laws that Congress has been compelled to pass laws to stop the IRS from implementing new and controversial regulations. Now the IRS bureaucracy seems to be challenging the U.S. Congress with a series of subtle moves and countermoves designed to allow the IRS to have its own way; it seems to be trying to "protect" the public treasury from what it perceives to be the "excessive generosity" of Congress.

It is against this background that this manual was conceived and written. With the public no longer believing their tax obligations are reasonable, and Internal Revenue behaving in an aggressive and self-serving way, many American taxpayers have become fighting mad and are finally ready to defend themselves. While most taxpayers might prefer to avoid any conflict with the IRS, they have no choice if their tax return is one of the millions selected for audit each year.

The purpose of *The Taxpayer's Audit Survival Manual* is to help you avoid an audit if you can, and to give you a fighting chance to survive Internal Revenue's steamroller tactics if you are audited.

In the movie "Patton," there is a scene where the general successfully trapped his German adversary, General Rommel. Patton stood up and yelled, "I read your book, you @#$%¢$*@!" Taxpayers who are serious about paying the least amount of taxes required by law should also take the time to become familiar with the strengths, weaknesses, and preferred tactics of their opponent—the IRS.

However, most books dealing with audit strategies are written for tax specialists and are difficult for a layman, without their technical background, to understand. Internal Revenue's own audit manuals, written for its staff, are onesided in viewpoint and are even more incomprehensible than the publications used by tax professionals. Internal Revenue, for obvious reasons, ignores the subject when educating the public on how to pay taxes promptly and efficiently. *Your Income Tax* (Publication 17) and the *Tax Guide for Small Business* (Publication 334), IRS' "bestsellers" on the income tax, are both 200-page works, but each devotes only a single page to the subject of audits and appeals.

In this book, we have tried to make the obscure but important topic of tax audits understandable to the average taxpayer. We think we have succeeded.

A tax audit should be an educational experience, in terms of learning something useful for future tax planning and when preparing future tax returns. In this manual, we have attempted to provide you with audit experience in advance, to increase the effectiveness of your tax planning and your preparation for future audits, and to allow you to survive unavoidable audits with as little damage as possible.

We would like to invite readers of this manual with audit experiences (both positive and negative) to communicate them to us for possible use in future editions of this manual. If you discover that the manual's suggestions need modification, or are inappropriate in certain situations, please call that to our attention. However, as much as we would like to, we can't promise to correspond with readers about their personal tax problems. Any information you would like to offer should be sent to us at Enterprise Publishing, Inc., 725 Market Street, Wilmington, Delaware 19801.

Lastly, we would like to express our appreciation to our original publisher, Robert Kephart, and to our present publisher, Enterprise Publishing, Inc., for recognizing the need for such a work.

Vernon K. Jacobs
Prairie Village, KS

Charles W. Schoeneman
Washington, DC

The Audit Lottery 1

Every year, the U.S. Internal Revenue Service runs a great lottery. Your income tax return, your Form 1040, is your lottery ticket and your tax payments are your entry fee. April 15th is the deadline, but late entries are permitted.

Now this lottery is different than most; in a sense it is actually a "reverse lottery." The minority whose tickets are selected become the losers; the winners are the majority whose entries are ignored.

This lottery has other interesting features. Though participation is compulsory, most players are blissfully unaware that they have even entered. Even the winners, since they are ignored, often remain ignorant of their good luck. Only the losers have any sense of involvement, for they must pay the prize money.

The odds are much lower than in most sweepstakes. Instead of 100,000-to-one or 1,000-to-one odds against winning, this lottery's odds are about 45-to-one *in favor of winning,* against having your ticket picked at all.

This strange event, of course, is what tax professionals have nicknamed the "audit lottery." The losers have their tax returns selected for audit; the winners' returns and tax payments are accepted by Internal Revenue without comment.

This manual is about the great annual IRS audit lottery and the rules—both written and unwritten—by which it is played. It's goal is to help you become a better player, understanding the game well enough to skirt the traps set for the unwary by the game's organizers. Reading this book should help a taxpayer become a semi-pro, skillful enough, with a little luck, to avoid most of the penalties charged novices for playing foolishly. With a better understanding of the audit system, the reader will increase his confidence in his own abilities, and lose much of his fear of his opponent, the IRS. As in every other game, a higher level of skill and confidence should materially increase your chances of winning.

Let's start with some basics.

An Adversary System

The U.S. tax system is basically an adversary system. Taxpayers are on one side, and the IRS on the other.

There are several things the Internal Revenue Service is and one thing it isn't. It isn't the taxpayer's friend. The word "service" in its name is misleading. It may perform a service for Congress, or for the Treasury, but not for an individual taxpayer.

The IRS is a huge bureaucracy, 85,000 strong, dedicated to obtaining as much of the national wealth, with as little disturbance or public fuss, as possible.

The successful player always thinks of Internal Revenue as his opponent, the other team, and remembers that it plays for money, his money.

Psyching the Taxpayer

Advanced players of any sport always play a mental game as much as a physical one. They win because they prepare their opponents to lose.

The IRS does its best to "psych out" the taxpayer. Amercans are encouraged to be good citizens, to freely ante up their money for patriotic reasons.

Mortimer Caplin, a former IRS Commissioner, once stated, "Our tax system is based on individual self-assessment and voluntary compliance. The vitality of the system hinges on the good faith of the American people and their willingness to report their income accurately. This good faith is largely dependent upon the public's general confidence that our tax laws are fair, and that they are impartially and uniformly administered and enforced so that everyone is paying his just share."

Commissioner Caplin's staff wrote this for him back in the early 1960s. The bits about fairness and "everyone . . . paying his just share" have a different ring to them now. The American perception of government and fair play are not what they once were.

But Internal Revenue still uses much the same pattern, even internally. Here is a quote from a recent audit manual: "The mission of the Internal Revenue Service is to encourage and achieve the highest possible degree of voluntary compliance with the tax laws and regulations and to maintain the highest degree of public confidence in the integrity and efficiency of the Service."

Perhaps a more useful way to think of the IRS is as "administrator" of the national tax laws. Without conscience, it acts as a servant of Congress, always trying to be as efficient as possible within the limits of the resources allowed it.

To achieve the "highest possible degree of voluntary compliance" that it often speaks of requires that the taxpaying public willingly and accurately assess their own taxes. With this in mind, the IRS instructs and communicates with the public, checks up on areas of non-compliance, does whatever is necessary to enforce the tax law. Its main enforcement tools are tax audits, the use of penalties for delinquents, a vigorous collection effort, and the investigation (with the threat of punishment) of anyone not playing by its rules.

Internal Revenue always tries to maintain an image of efficiency. As will become clear as we progress, the IRS is not always the perfect clerk; it is sometimes overwhelmed by the immensity of its paperwork chores.

And when there is no paperwork at all, Internal Revenue is largely impotent. Only a small fraction of those who escape paying taxes by their efforts in the "underground economy," that deals only in cash, ever come to the attention of the IRS.

To help maintain its reputation for knowing all, being everywhere, and catching every delinquent, the IRS uses publicity, bragging about those it does catch. Every year, in the late winter and early spring, when taxpayers are thinking about their taxes, the IRS mounts a publicity campaign. Information is sent to the media about the IRS' computer systems, and on tax cases it has won that have guaranteed intimidation value. Newspapers everywhere carry reports of taxpayers who have been caught in various illegal tax evasion schemes and severely punished as a result of IRS enforcement programs.

Audits and Examinations

Internal Revenue relies heavily on the audit process to carry the threat to the taxpayer, too. A notification of audit is the long arm of the IRS tapping a taxpayer on the shoulder.

The Internal Revenue Service, though, perhaps to increase the mystery and decrease the dread, does not commonly use the word "audit" in its communications with the citizenry. Instead, it notifies them that their tax returns have been selected for "examination."

Inside the service, though, there are "Audit Technique Handbooks," "field audits," and "tax auditors." Until the latest IRS reorganization, there was an "Audit Division," now called the "Examination Division." IRS bigwigs still fondly refer to this division as their "audit machine," even though it now conducts "examinations."

Throughout this book, the words "audit" and "examination" are used interchangeably. Whatever they are called, audits are a very essential part of this nation's income tax collection arrangements.

Civil vs. Criminal Audits

Most tax returns that are examined are subject to "civil audits." At issue are matters of quantity (how big a deduction is allowable or provable), and interpretation of the tax law (always an interesting point with the IRS). A taxpayer undergoing a civil audit is, in IRS' view, basically playing fair. IRS rules and regulations are generally being observed even if the taxpayer stretches them a bit. Internal Revenue's object in this type of audit is only to pick up some additional tax revenue and possibly a few penalty charges and a lot of interest.

If the taxpayer plays too rough, entering into the areas of tax evasion or fraud, Internal Revenue plays the game rougher too. The objective now becomes punishment *and* the collection of extra taxes and heavy penalties. Taxpayers in this category are likely to be subjected to a "criminal audit." If the IRS can prove any of a number of "tax crimes," the taxpayer is liable for fines, and possibly

imprisonment, besides the additional taxes assessed.

Any audit, civil or criminal, is a negative, no-win, guilt-inducing situation for a taxpayer. More than money is involved. The burden of proof is on the taxpayer in an audit situation; he is considered guilty, or at least suspect, until he justifies his tax self-assessment to the IRS auditor. Even if no additional tax liability is found, there are costs involved for the taxpayer's time spent on the audit, and for the expense of any professional accounting or legal help needed.

And once audited, there is always the threat of future audits, for the IRS often returns to shake a tree where it has found fruit in prior years.

Tax Avoidance, Evasion, and Rebellion

Tax "avoidance," the arranging of your business and personal affairs so as to minimize liability for taxes, is completely legal.

The most quoted explanation of this point by one of this country's most famous judges states, "Over and over again the courts have said that there is nothing sinister in so arranging one's affairs as to keep taxes as low as possible. Everybody does so, rich or poor; and all do right, for nobody owes any public duty to pay more than the law demands; taxes are enforced exactions, not voluntary contributions. To demand more in the name of morals is mere cant." Judge Learned Hand wrote these words, more than 30 years ago. (*Commissioner vs. Newman*, 159 F. 2nd 848, 2d Circ. 1947)

There are many devices available to help avoid taxes legally. Among those sanctioned by Internal Revenue and the tax laws are various tax shelters, accelerated depreciation, and trusts of many types. Tax avoidance is the passive way, but the wisest way to pay less tax. Successful tax avoiders study the rules of the game, seek professional coaching when necessary, and are usually better than average players of the audit game.

Tax "evasion" is another matter entirely. Evaders use trickery, omission, fraud (they lie on their tax returns), and stealth to cut their apparent tax liability. Tax evasion is illegal, though the line between aggressive tax avoidance and low-key evasion can be vague at times. Tax evaders, if caught, are punished by the other team's rules. Past due taxes are likely to become due in one lump sum, together with stiff penalties and fines. Sometimes, convicted evaders are sentenced to prison terms.

Tax "rebellion" is the out-and-out refusal to pay taxes. Tax rebels usually attempt to flaunt their resistance, and play by their own interpretations of the rules. They argue legalistically over rights and Constitutional issues. In the end, though, they are forced to turn to the courts, hoping for justice in yet another government-controlled game.

If the inequalities and the injustices of our present tax system make you rage, perhaps you should channel some of the emotional energy into the "tax reform" movement. The problems of cutting one's personal tax exposure and of reforming the entire tax system are entirely different matters. Become first a successful "avoider" and then a "reformer."

If the urge to become a martyr burns in your blood, this manual is probably not for you. Perhaps you should put it down and find instead one of the more rabid tracts on tax rebellion.

About This Manual

One purpose of this manual is to help a taxpayer avoid an audit whenever possible. Another is to help the reader, if subjected to a tax examination, to get through it smoothly and painlessly.

As befits a book about a reverse lottery, losing will be covered before winning, and in greater detail. One reason, of course, is that nothing much happens to winners of the audit lottery. More basic is that a taxpayer must understand why and how audits are conducted before effective defensive measures can be taken.

Essential to an understanding of the IRS audit system is to know how tax returns are chosen for audit, or what tags a return for further attention. An entire chapter is devoted to this important subject.

Another introductory chapter covers the organization and functions of the IRS and describes the various types of tax agents a taxpayer is likely to face. In any context, be it war, bridge, tennis or taxes, it is a good idea to know the opponent's strengths and weaknesses.

There are several distinctly different levels of audit. Several chapters familiarize the reader with each type in turn. Advice is also given on countering IRS moves in the audit process to retain as much control as possible.

Internal Revenue's investigation and collection divisions have a deservedly tough reputation. The likely tactics of each, and taxpayer rights while being investigated or forced to pay, are also covered. There are two chapters that explain the proccesses by which an Internal Revenue decision can be appealed and, perhaps, reversed.

There is no 100 percent sure way to avoid the unwelcome attentions of an Internal Revenue auditor. However, there are some things a taxpayer can do to maintain a low profile and to minimize the chances of his return being picked for scrutiny. These are explained in a final section.

By the time the reader finishes this manual, he will have enough knowledge to be able to face a tax examination with reasonable calmness and confidence. He will also understand what steps he might take to help avoid such unpleasantness in the future.

In short, he will be a member of a minority, one of the small band of taxpayers who actually understand the audit process.

**The Tax Dollar
Where It Came From
Fiscal Year 1978 (Gross Collections)**

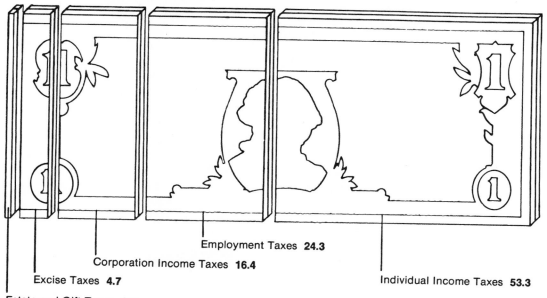

Employment Taxes **24.3**

Corporation Income Taxes **16.4**

Individual Income Taxes **53.3**

Excise Taxes **4.7**

Estate and Gift Taxes **1.3**

**The Tax Dollar
Where It Came From
Fiscal Year 1978 (Net Collections)**

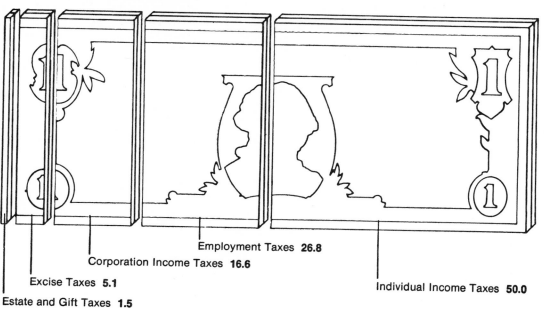

Employment Taxes **26.8**

Corporation Income Taxes **16.6**

Individual Income Taxes **50.0**

Excise Taxes **5.1**

Estate and Gift Taxes **1.5**

The Selection Process 2

In any lottery, the audit lottery included, the element of luck is present. In Internal Revenue's lottery, however, factors other than pure chance are also important. For example, where you reside can affect your chances of being picked.

In 1977, there were 85,623,810 taxpayers who filed individual tax returns, their official entries in the IRS raffle. Over the next year, 1,845,242 of these were audited. This means that 97.84 percent of those who filed won at the audit game and were ignored, at least temporarily. (Their returns could be audited in combination with other years' returns at a later date.) Only 2.16 percent lost and were audited. Thus, the overall random odds against a particular return being examined were about 45-to-one. These odds, in terms of all types and classes of individual returns, will remain about the same for the foreseeable future.

Primarily, this is because the IRS simply does not have the capability, the trained manpower to audit a higher percentage of the returns filed. During the year we are using as an example, Internal Revenue had an average of only 13,927 field auditors and 4,617 office auditors. (The distinction will be explained later.) Office auditors average 3.3 hours and field auditors 17.3 hours per return. This means that, at a maximum, the inside people could handle an average of 10 to 12 cases per week, and the outside men only about two.

But these are only ideal maximums. If it is anything, the Internal Revenue Service is a bureaucracy, afflicted with all the problems of any large organization. Production (the number of audits conducted) is affected by all the usual bureaucratic time-eaters: meetings, travel time, sick days, coffee breaks, broken appointments, internal paperwork, training sessions, and so on. Because of this, perhaps only 45 percent of an average auditor's time is spent in actual auditing.

To make up for this slippage and for its relative lack of auditing power compared with its task in hand, the IRS has turned to computers on a massive scale. It uses the computer as a tool to help select those returns on which it believes its auditors might spend their time most profitably.

Since 1969, the IRS has been using a computer-applied mathematical technique called "Discriminant Function." This process, usually called by its acronym, DIF, is used to identify those returns the IRS thinks most likely to yield additional taxes if audited.

TCMP

To develop the formulas used in the DIF selection process, the IRS has relied on information generated by its "Taxpayer Compliance Measurement Program." Every two to four years, approximately 50,000 tax returns are subjected to a rigorous "compliance" audit, to provide data for analysis and for further refinement of the DIF selection formulas.

As we will see later on, it is possible to take steps to maintain a low profile and generally to minimize one's chances of being audited. However, such precautionary measures are ineffective against TCMP audits. Only raw luck counts in those years when TCMP audits are being conducted, since selection is an entirely random process.

For TCMP purposes, all individual returns are divided into 45 classes. These start out with the simplest, "non-business" 1040 returns with an Adjusted Gross Income under $10,000 that claim only a standard deduction. Returns that include a Schedule C or a Schedule F are in separate groupings. Classes are further segregated by Adjusted Gross Income, typically into "under $10,000," "$10,000 to $30,000," "$30,000 to $100,000," and "over $100,000" categories.

For each of the 45 classes, the number of returns needed to provide an adequate sample is decided by IRS statistical, research, and data processing people.

For example, one class is limited to 1040 returns with a Schedule C, that have an Adjusted Gross Income of under $10,000 on gross receipts of $100,000 or more. For calendar year 1976, it was judged that about 1,300 returns would be needed to sample this group. Since around 108,000 tax returns had been filed that fit this description, only 12 per thousand were needed as a sample.

The Rand Corporation's Table of Random Digits was used by the Statistics Division to select numbers representing the last three digits of taxpayers' Social Security numbers (SSN). Twelve three-digit numbers were selected for this particular class by a simple process depending solely on luck. These numbers were: 749, 095, 518, 343, 698, 940, 826, 508, 993, 853, 151 and 608.

Internal Revenue maintains a National Computer Center at Martinsburg, West Virginia which has taped data on every tax return filed. At the center, a program containing the randomly chosen numbers was run against tapes holding information on all of the 108,000 or so returns in this category. All returns on which the last three digits of the taxpayer's SSN matched the 12 unlucky numbers were selected.

A selection, using an identical process but different SSNs, was made from each of the 45 classes of returns. The National Center then produced a computer tape for each Regional Service Center. This tape contained identifying information on every return in that region to be included in the TCMP audit. District offices were then provided the specific returns by their service centers.

IRS district offices have no options but to complete their audits of these returns. They can neither drop nor add taxpayers to the TCMP Audit Program. The IRS National Office can give permission to delete a TCMP return, but this is done only under exceptional circumstances. A taxpayer under investigation for possible tax fraud, or on his death bed might be excluded.

All returns under this program are given an audit that explores all aspects of their potential tax liability, a more strenuous exam than normally used. And, of course, whenever possible, additional taxes are assessed.

Despite the fact that, once selected, there is no real way to avoid a TCMP audit, there is no point in worrying about the possibility. The odds are even more in your favor than with a regular audit. In the years that TCMP audits are conducted, only one taxpayer in about 1,750 will be picked for a compliance audit.

After a Return is Filed

Before any returns can be chosen for any type of audit, they must be processed at an

IRS Regional Service Center. There are 10 of these centers, at least one and sometimes two, in each of the seven IRS regions. All tax returns are mailed directly to one of these service centers.

Once a return is received at a service center, it is processed through a series of steps called "the pipeline." This is a massive clerical operation, helped along by automation whenever possible.

As might be expected, first the envelopes are counted and opened. Then the returns are sorted and separated by type. Any checks or money orders are first compared with the accompanying return, and then prepared for deposit in a Treasury bank account.

At this stage, the preparation for audit selection really begins. Each return is manually edited and coded for further computer processing. Coded data from each return is keyed into a computer. The computers check the arithmetic and perform a series of validity tests on the data. Now the center begins to generate information on those returns with questionable items. Follow-up audits of one sort or another will be performed on these. This will be done by either the service center itself or by one of the district offices. But more on that later.

To keep everyone happy with the withholding system and to keep this lucrative system working for the government, priority is now given to tax refunds. Checks for refunds are printed and mailed by a Treasury Department Disbursing Center, acting on information provided by the service center.

A surprising, perhaps shocking, number of taxpayers seem to use their friendly IRS system as a sort of savings bank, even though they earn no interest on their "savings." In 1978, the IRS paid out $39.6 billion to 69 million taxpayers. (The average individual refund was $495.)

The prevalence of this practice of "over-withholding" is perhaps one reason for Con-gress' lack of restraint in spending. Tempted by this $40 billion pool of loose change, the government uses it to increase its budget while postponing tax increases considered necessary to pay for the increased spending.

DIF in Action

Computer tapes carrying information on all tax returns filed are provided the Martinsburg National Computer Center by the various Regional Service Centers. These tapes are the raw material for the DIF system of picking returns with a high audit potential.

Internal Revenue supplies information to the interested public on its Taxpayer Compliance Measurement Program (TCMP), that provides the background research for the DIF screening formulas. The operation of DIF itself is highly sensitive and secret to the IRS, mainly because of its success. In 1968, the year before DIF became operational, no tax change was recommended for 43 percent of the returns examined. Using the DIF selection system, IRS audits have definitely generated more tax assessments; the critical "no tax change" figure is now down to 24 percent.

Understandably, the IRS is reluctant to compromise a highly successful program by revealing the details of its formulas even to the General Accounting Office, a sister agency. It is known, however, that a different formula exists for each class of tax return. DIF classes are organized similarly to the 45 TCMP classes, but are much broader in scope since there are only 10 of them:

DIF Formula

Audit Class
1. Low nonbusiness—Standard (adjusted gross income less than $10,000) excluding returns with interest and dividends of more than $200, other income, or adjustments to income.

2. Low nonbusiness—Itemized (adjusted gross income less than $10,000) includ-

Pipeline   At the ten Regional Service Centers

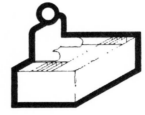

Envelopes are opened and counted

Returns are sorted by type of return

Tax returns and accompanying checks are compared.

Returns are edited and coded for computer processing.

Tax return information is fed into the computer

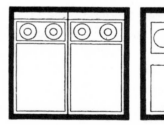

IRS computers perform validity checks on tax returns

Refund checks are printed by Treasury Department Disbursing Center

Once a tax return reaches one of ten IRS Service Centers, it travels through a series of processing steps known as "the pipeline." While many parts of the pipeline shown here are automated for faster processing and faster refunds, people are involved every step of the way.

ing returns with standard deductions and with interest and dividends of more than $200, other income, or adjustments to income.

3. Low business—Schedule C (adjusted gross income less than $10,000).
4. Low business—Schedule F (adjusted gross income less than $10,000).
5. Medium nonbusiness—(adjusted gross income of $10,000 but less than $50,000).
6. Medium business—Schedule C (adjusted gross income of $10,000 but less than $30,000).
7. Medium business—Schedule F (adjusted gross income of $10,000 but less than $30,000).
8. High nonbusiness—(adjusted gross income of $50,000 or more).
9. High business—Schedule C (adjusted gross income of $30,000 or more).
10. High business—Schedule F (adjusted gross income of $30,000 or more).

It is not necessary to know the actual formulas to surmise what the IRS is looking for. TCMP audits generate a great deal of data. It is relatively easy for the IRS to establish what represents acceptable limits for each class of return, and to express the norms in terms of mathematical ratios. If a deduction falls within certain boundaries, it probably represents a legitimate claim. Anything exceeding the established limits for a certain class of return represents a deviation worth pursuing further.

As an over-simplified example, consider the following. Two returns might each claim a charitable donation deduction totaling $1,500. One is a joint return with no dependents and an adjusted gross income of over $50,000. The second return has an AGI of less than $10,000 and claims a total of seven exemptions. On both returns the charitable deduction

is within the legally allowable 20 percent of the AGI. However, TCMP audits will have certainly verified that few lower-bracket taxpayers with seven mouths to feed can afford charitable contributions of this size.

As a consequence, because $1,500 is well outside the limits for this class of return, the computer will flag the lower-income return for audit. While the $1,500 deduction may be lawful, there is also a fair chance that it is not real; the taxpayer will be asked to produce proof.

For very practical reasons, Internal Revenue is very quiet about its DIF formulas, its ratios, its norms, its acceptable limits.

To use a fictitious example, suppose that DIF formulas allowed charitable contributions up to 2.1 percent of AGI. Once such a ratio became publicized, aggressive tax preparers everywhere would increase their clients' deductions to just under the limit knowing that, legitimate or not, such claims would not upset the computer. Obviously, to keep DIF effective, secrecy remains the IRS's best defense.

Application of the DIF system is less mysterious, though. Using computers, tapes containing the tax return data provided by the Regional Service Centers are run against the magical DIF formulas. This calculates a score for each return; the higher the score, the higher the probability of a tax increase upon audit. For each category, a cutting score is determined. Returns scoring below this point will not be examined under the DIF audit program. Returns with a score above the critical point are listed on a special DIF inventory file.

Tapes listing returns on the DIF inventory file are sent back to the service center where the original tax forms have been held. Each service center then provides its district offices with a weekly inventory listing, by category, of highscore returns that are available for audit.

At District Office Level

Using this inventory, the district office now orders returns for possible audit. When the returns arrive at the district office, they undergo screening by a "classifier," a highly experienced agent who reviews each return. Particular attention is paid to the detailed schedules supporting the deductions questioned by the computers in West Virginia. Some tax returns are dropped from further scrutiny at this point because, in the opinion of the classifier, they do not warrant an audit. None may be added at this stage.

Classifiers have been given generally high marks for their impartiality. A General Accounting Office report in 1976 said, "Our interviews with classifiers and our observations of returns being classified disclosed no evidence that returns were being arbitrarily or capriciously selected for audit under the DIF system. All evidence indicated that returns selected for audit under this system were selected because, in the classifier's best judgment, they warranted audit." There is no reason to believe that their work is still not fairly performed.

After the classifier has finished, the remaining returns are then made available for assignment to specific auditors. As a result of this screening arrangement, the auditor ultimately performing an examination is not the person who classified and selected the return for audit. However, at a later stage, an auditor himself could be responsible for picking a return for audit even though it wasn't in a DIF batch at all. (This exception will be explained later.)

All returns that survive this double screening, computer and human, may not be audited, however. Manpower, auditor time, becomes a factor. Each district office has a personnel budget with its available "staff-years" distributed by category and type of audit. Some taxpayers luck out simply because there are not enough auditors to go around.

Other District Office Audits

Audits on returns selected under the DIF system constitute about 70 percent of the workload at an average district office. There are several other types of returns that are audited at this level.

Many taxpayers utilize professional help in completing their return. Some tax preparers have built their practice by word-of-mouth referrals, by their reputation for always getting big refunds on the returns they complete. The name of the game, of course, is large deductions, documented or not. A good reputation with the form-filing public is not necessarily a good reputation at the local IRS office. Internal Revenue has a formal program that concentrates on tax preparers of ill-repute, suspected of fraudulent practices. An individual's return may be targeted for audit simply because it was processed by a tax preparer the IRS considers too aggressive with deductions.

Taxpayers may file an amended tax return any time within three years of the date their original return was filed. There is even a special form for the purpose, Form 1040X. A return may be amended in order to pay additional taxes. More likely, an amended return will be in the taxpayer's favor, filed to claim deductions or credits not taken on the original, and to ask for a refund.

Of all the various sorts of tax returns, amended returns stand the highest chance of an audit. Classifiers screen all amended returns carefully, and divide them into those with high, average, or low audit potential. Audit potential is, of course, the chance to assess more taxes. All amended returns of high potential are audited; 10 percent of the low-potential amended returns are examined as a spot check.

Audits are also initiated by the district office on information reported by third parties. This may be a direct lead from an informant who, incidentally, may be paid a reward of up to 10 percent of the additional taxes assessed. Leads may also come indirectly, perhaps from items on another tax return. For example, payments made in cash and claimed as legitimate deductions by another taxpayer could prompt the IRS to check to see if the recipient included the cash as part of his reported income.

"Related pickups" are audits made to check the validity of another taxpayer's claims. Examples would be to check a brother's or sister's return to see which family members claimed an aged parent as a deduction, or to audit all partners to verify the return of one member of a partnership. Returns of employers, or even employees, of a taxpayer might also be audited as "related pickups."

The General Accounting Office made the following observation about this program: "To obtain a related return, the examiner prepares a requisition which must be approved by his immediate supervisor. On the requisition, he indicates by a code number why he is requesting the return. . . . The examiner is not required to provide any more information to justify his request. If the requisition is approved, the service center will forward the return directly to the examiner."

"Multi-year audits" are examinations of returns filed in past years by the same taxpayer. An assessment made against a taxpayer for one year might send the IRS scurrying back to prior returns to look for the same weak spot. With little extra effort the auditor might pick up two or three times as much new tax money. Investment losses carried forward might lead an auditor to check the treatment of the losses in prior years. To obtain the desired returns, the auditor follows the same relatively lax procedures described previously for "related pickups."

There are few safeguards against an auditor who thinks a particular taxpayer known to him should be audited. The GAO, Congress's toothless watchdog, spotted the potential for abuse years ago. It noted that "The requisition prepared by the examiner to obtain these returns contains a code but no written explanation why the examiner needs the return and thus gives management (the group manager, the district review staff, and the internal audit staff) little basis for evaluating that need." The GAO recommended that examiners be required to justify their requests for other returns with written explanations, but the IRS resisted the suggestion.

Despite the opportunity, at a minimum, for violation of a taxpayer's financial privacy, the IRS denied there was a problem needing correction. However, it is probably silly for any taxpayer to pretend to financial modesty with the IRS anyway, given its other powers to obtain information.

In addition, every district does audits that do not fit any of the above categories. TCMP audits, 50,000 or so done by the 58 district offices, are probably the most numerous miscellaneous type of audit. Test audits are occasionally run on a limited basis by one or two district offices to check taxpayer reporting of certain items. In 1979, the IRS was reportedly spot-checking to see if homeowners who sold their homes reported the sales correctly on their returns. The results of such an audit series could lead to new procedures to tighten up a particular reporting area.

There are also "training audits," which the IRS does not publicize but which tax return preparers certainly know about. A district office will select relatively simple itemized returns, probably from the DIF inventory, to teach their trainees how to make a taxpayer sweat.

Tax fraud investigations are also included in this "miscellaneous audit" category.

Service Center Screening

Much of the work of the Regional Service Centers revolves around the routine processing of tax returns. Data is fed to the National Computer Center, computerized inventories of returns available for audit are provided the district offices, refunds are issued, and tax returns are stored awaiting final disposition.

But the Regional Service Centers are also involved in the selection of tax returns for further examination.

Unallowable Items

Returns singled out by the DIF system are those on which the itemized deductions exceed what IRS considers the reasonable limits. Service centers run a comparable effort, called the "Unallowable Items" program. This project handles items that, to quote the Internal Revenue Manual, "are unallowable by law and not merely questionable."

During the center's initial processing of tax returns, those with an item on the current Unallowable Items list will be culled out, either by computer or upon manual review. A form letter is then sent, informing the taxpayer that a particular item is being disallowed. The tax is recomputed, and the taxpayer either billed or the refund due cut to reflect the adjustment.

The Unallowable Items master list changes from time to time to reflect revisions of the tax law and changes in the tax forms in use. Generally, though, the list is a long one. Most items pertain only to returns with itemized deductions.

The Unallowable Items list from the 1979 IRS Manual is provided in the back of this manual as Appendix 1. It should be useful as a check list.

Head of Household Program

Those returns in which the special tax table or computations for "Unmarried Head of Household" are used are scrutinized to see that the taxpayer meets the tests for this filing status.

Generally, any taxpayer claiming only one exemption is suspect if he or she files as "head of household." A form letter requesting more information will also be sent if the name of a "qualifying" person is not listed in the proper space on Form 1040.

This is a category in which the IRS has been making a concentrated effort to insure compliance. As the tax laws gradually change, or as areas of abuse are identified, other items will receive similar heavy attention from the IRS.

Information Returns

This is an area with which Internal Revenue is having trouble, but still making an effort.

An "Information Return" is used to report wages, dividends, interest, and other miscellaneous income such as royalties, to the IRS. In 1978, 484 million information returns were sent to the IRS. Over 265 million of these reports were received on computer tape. These, ready to use on IRS computers, were almost all matched with the master file of taxpayers.

The rest, on paper forms, present an enormous clerical problem to Internal Revenue. The IRS Annual Report admits that only about 15 percent of these were successfully checked against other records. Needless to say, the IRS has a program to encourage magnetic reporting from those organizations with computer capability.

Matching information returns with reported income creates yet another inventory file of taxpayers possibly subject to audit. The examination division draws returns listed on this file—if the audit potential is high enough and if the district has audit personnel available.

Multiple Filers

Apparent "multiple filers" are checked out; an investigation is started if two or more returns carrying the same Social Security identification number are filed in the same year.

In years past, before Internal Revenue's National Computer Center was fully operational, multiple filing presented an opportunity for the criminally inclined to make some serious money at the expense of the Treasury. Duplicate tax returns, each claiming a refund and providing a copy of a legitimate W-2, would be filed in each of several regions. There were many variations on this dodge, including using mail-forwarding addresses, W-2 forms of real but unsuspecting taxpayers, and even completely false names and W-2s. With the IRS unable to compare returns scattered across the nation, the perpetrators were often successful. Only excessive greed on the filer's part, or blind luck for the IRS, occasionally aroused suspicion and caused 10 or 20 or more returns to be physically picked out of tens of millions and compared.

Multiple filing does not lead to a form letter, or even a conventional audit. The service centers turn their information over to the IRS Criminal Investigation Division. Vigorous follow-ups are conducted, often in coordination with the FBI and the Postal Inspection Service. Identification of multiple filers usually leads to their arrest and some time in a federal penitentiary. (Some multiple filers are already there; inmates have been reported as among the most active multiple filers.)

Internal Revenue's rapid and routine issuance of refund checks probably still represents a temptation to many. Multiple filing is probably on the decrease because of the IRS's increased computer capability.

Other Service Center Activities

The effort against multiple filers is only one of several miscellaneous categories of audit activity in which Regional Service Centers are active.

There is a "Federal-State Cooperative Audit Program." State tax agencies send audit reports to their local service center for comparison with federal tax returns. Sometimes the Social Security Administration suspects that a taxpayer is self-employed and has unreported income. This is reported to the IRS through a service center.

Service centers also process claims for refunds on amended returns that are simple enough to be resolved through the mails, or by an examination of the documents already on file at the center.

Your Chances of Audit

At the beginning of this chapter, it was stated that only 2.16 percent of the individual tax returns filed for 1977 were given any type of audit. It is only appropriate that the chapter end by giving you some idea of what the general odds are for your return.

The following figures were taken from Internal Revenue's 1978 Annual Report, the most recent year for which a complete tally is available. A "business" return is one filed with a Schedule C or a Schedule F attached. A breakdown on the types of examinations given each class of return is also included. The dollar amounts are for Adjusted Gross Income (AGI) levels.

Returns Filed, Examinations and Examination Coverage

| | Returns Filed | Returns Examined Fiscal Year 1978 | | | | |
	Calendar Year 1977	Revenue Agents	Tax Auditors	Service Center	Total	Percent Coverage
Individual Returns Total	85,623,810	306,433	1,369,419	169,390	1,845,242	2.16
Form 1040 Standard Deduction	27,901,848	7,882	171,303	6,959	186,144	.67
Itemized Returns:						
Non-business						
Under $10,000	11,992,130	20,823	286,824	40,337	347,984	2.90
$10,000 to $15,000	12,853,606	21,416	267,575	47,296	334,817	2.60
$15,000 to $50,000	21,646,283	49,322	458,369	63,539	571,230	2.64
Over $50,000	799,885	59,493	22,675	1,047	83,215	10.40
Business						
Under $10,000	4,311,616	39,071	98,497	3,677	141,245	3.28
$10,000 to $30,000	4,910,803	46,934	46,654	6,319	99,907	2.03
Over $30,000	1,207,639	61,492	17,522	1,686	80,700	6.68

Editor's note: It should be noted that corporate returns have a much greater likelihood of audit.

The Taxpayer's Opponent 3

There are about 220 million people who live in the United States. Every year, this mighty crowd files over 140 million tax returns of all types with the Internal Revenue Service. And, it must be remembered, each return is a fairly complicated piece of paper.

To cope with this mind-boggling mass of paperwork, the IRS has about 85,000 employees and spends about $2 billion to collect about $400 billion. It costs the IRS just under 50 cents to obtain $100 from the taxpaying public.

Abraham Lincoln is a saint to many people, but there was a bit of the devil in him too. The origins of the Internal Revenue Service date back to a bill he signed on July 1, 1862, creating the post of Internal Revenue Commissioner. Until the necessity of financing the Civil War, or the War of Secession if you prefer, the federal government had managed to get by nicely on its income from customs duties, the sale of federal lands, and excise taxes. The new law added may taxes. Among other things, it provided for levies on income, progressive rates of taxation, and even tax withholding, the foundation of our current tax system.

The first commissioner was George S. Boutwell, a lawyer and prominent Republican from Massachusetts. He started work on July 17, 1862 with one clerk.

Commissioner Boutwell remained in office only until March of 1863, but he got Internal Revenue off to a roaring start. By January 1863, he had over 6,800 employees. The cutting edge of his force were "assessors" who were paid a daily rate for their work, and "collectors" who received a commission on the taxes they gathered. Some worked as "tax contractors" and were paid 50 percent commission on their collections. By 1866, tax collections were running $300 million a year.

The income tax was dropped in 1872, but revived in 1894. In 1895, the U.S. Supreme Court ruled that a personal income tax was unconstitutional because, as a "direct" tax, it was not apportioned among the states according to their populations.

The original power of Congress to tax was clearly stated in the first paragraph of Section 8, Article I of the Constitution, even though it does not specifically authorize a tax on personal income. To quote: "The Congress shall have Power To lay and collect taxes, Duties, Imports and Excises, to pay the Debts and provide for the common Defence and general Welfare of the Untied States; but all Duties, Imports and excises shall be uniform through the United States. . . ."

The word "uniform" was one of the sticking points for an income tax. Another question was whether an income tax was a "direct" tax, which Sections 2 and 9 of Article I required to be apportioned. The Supreme Court held that it was a "direct" tax, and hence unconstitutional as applied to individuals. After much campaigning and debate, this alleged oversight by the framers of the Constitution was remedied by the 16th Amendment to the Constitution. It was ratified in 1913, just in time to help finance World War I. It reads as follows: "The Congress shall have power to lay and collect taxes on incomes, from whatever source derived, without apportionment among the several States, and without regard to any census or enumeration." Internal Revenue promptly added a "Personal Income Tax Division."

The Revenue Act of 1916 ushered in a new era of taxation. Until then, taxes were primarily to raise revenue for the costs of government. The rich paid more taxes than the poor, but mainly because exemptions were high enough to allow wage earners to pay little or no income tax; tax rates were also generally quite flat. The 1916 law levied an estate tax for the first time, to penalize the passing of wealth from one generation to the next. Taxes started to become an instrument of social change, transferring resources from one segment of the citizenry to another.

Taxes were greater than ever during World War I. In 1918, federal tax receipts were $3.6 billion, a significant rise from 1917's collections of $809 million. Income tax rates ran as high as 77 percent for some upper-income taxpayers.

Rates were cut in the 1920s, but raised again during the Depression years, to help pay for Franklin D. Roosevelt's social experiments and to help offset a decline in federal revenues caused by a declining national income. In 1939, the first tax "code" was enacted. By 1941, with Roosevelt still president, collections were up to $7.4 billion annually.

Administration and collection are the main problems of a mass income tax system. The needs of World War II led to the Current Tax Payments Act of 1943, which forced employers to withhold taxes from the wages of their employees. Withholding became the key to successsfully collecting high rates of income taxes from lower-income taxpayers; revenues for 1945 were $45 billion.

Federal tax revenues have continued to grow steadily ever since. In 1954, the Code we use now was enacted; remarkably, the framework for taxing individuals, partnerships, and corporations enacted then has not changed since, though the rules have. The $100 billion mark in revenues from income taxes was passed in 1963, the $200 billion milestone by 1972. The end is not yet in sight; receipts for 1981 will approach or exceed $500 billion.

The Organization

Through all of this, the size of the Internal Revenue Service (before 1954, it was the "Bureau") increased too. Its work force did not grow at the same rate its collections increased. The IRS' personnel growth rate more nearly parallels the expansion of the American population. In 1963, with collections at $105 billion and with 189 million Americans, Internal Revenue employed just under 60,000 people. By 1973, the population had hit 208 million and IRS personnel 68,000, though revenues climbed to $209 billion. Tax revenues doubled again by 1978 (in half the time of the previous doubling), the population climbed to 219 million, but Internal Revenue increased its staff by only 17,000.

Inflation, which leads to higher dollar incomes pushing people into higher tax brackets, is to blame for much of the apparent success of the IRS's collections. But there has also been a real increase in efficiency because of the adoption of computers and better management methods.

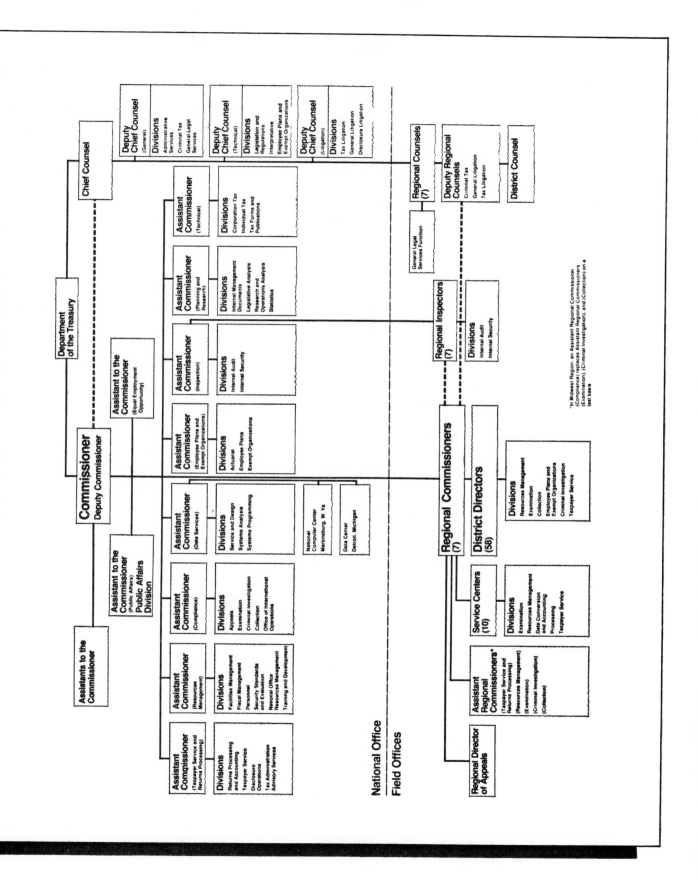

Internal Revenue seems to constantly reorganize itself in search of better management control of the tax collection process. The results of the most recent effort, in 1978, are displayed on the organizational chart in this chapter.

There are basically three organizational levels within the IRS: the National Office, Regions, and Districts.

The National Office is organized on functional lines. Reporting to the commissioner's office are eight Assistant Commissioners and a Chief Counsel. Each Assistant Commissioner is responsible for one functional area: Taxpayer Service and Returns Processing; Compliance; Resources Management (housekeeping, personnel, training, and so on); Data Services (the computer people); Employee Plans and Exempt Organizations (pension plans and foundations); Inspection (IRS internal audit and security); Planning and Research; or Technical.

"Compliance" is the headquarters unit supervising the Examination, Criminal Investigation, Collection, and Appeals Divisions. These are the only IRS functions that a taxpayer being audited will normally have any contact with.

The Chief Counsel supervises all legal functions, including representing the IRS in Tax Court. The job of representing the IRS before other federal courts against taxpayers making an appeal is done, however, by the Justice Department (usually the Tax Division), sometimes called the "Commissioner's lawyers."

The IRS's National Computer Center at Martinsburg is considered part of the National Office and is controlled by the Assistant Commissioner for Data Services.

Regions and Districts

A Regional Commissioner is responsible for each of the seven IRS regions. Under him

are Assistant Regional Commissioners who each supervise one division: Taxpayer Service and Returns Processing; Resources Management, Examination; Criminal Investigation; or Collection. In each region, there is also a Regional Director of Appeals. Each region has its own computer-equipped Regional Service Center and some regions have two.

Regions are further broken down into districts whose boundaries usually follow state lines, each headed by a District Director. There are 58 districts in all, with from seven to 13 in any particular region.

Districts are concerned largely with taxpayer service and taxpayer compliance. Taxpayer service means forms and information; compliance mainly examination, investigation and collection.

District offices are most often located in the larger cities of a region; the few exceptions are where a district office is located in a Regional Service Center in a suburb of a major city. Each district also has several branch offices, strategically placed in population centers within its area.

The Front Line

Taxpayer compliance is enforced by IRS's Examination, Criminal Investigation, and Collection Divisions. They carry on the never-ending battle to enforce the federal tax laws and Internal Revenue's many regulations. They try to collect as much extra tax money as legally possible. Each division has its own function and its own specialized troops. There is a detachment from each division in every district and each branch office.

Until the latest reorganization, the Examination Division was called the "Audit Division." There are two types of tax examiners in this division. "Tax auditors," sometimes called "office auditors," perform examinations on less complicated tax returns in an IRS office. "Revenue agents" handle the more

Map of the Regions, Districts, and Service Centers

Key:

⊛ Commissioner of Internal Revenue (Washington, D.C.)

○ District Director

★ National Computer Center (Martinsburg, W. Va.)

—— Regional Boundary

■ Regional Commissioner

● Service Center

◆ IRS Data Center (Detroit, Mich.)

- - - - District Boundary

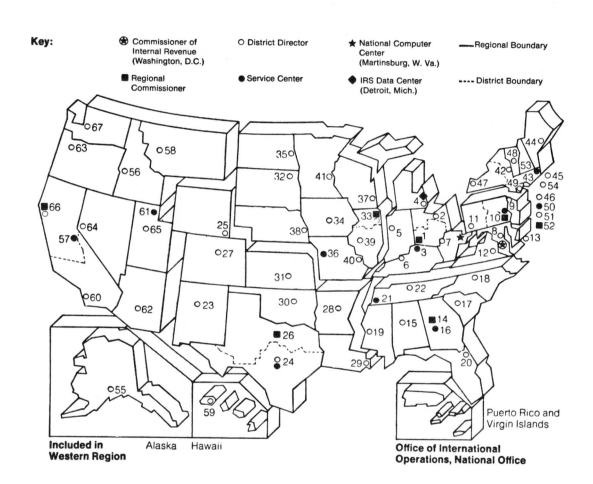

Included in Western Region   Alaska   Hawaii

Puerto Rico and Virgin Islands

Office of International Operations, National Office

Region and District Legend:

Central Region
1 Cincinnati, Ohio
2 Cleveland, Ohio
3 Covington, KY. (Cincinnati, SC)
4 Detroit, Mich.
5 Indianapolis, Ind.
6 Louisville, Ky.
7 Parkersburg, W. Va.

Mid-Atlantic Region
8 Baltimore, Md.
9 Newark, N.J.
10 Philadelphia, Pa.
11 Pittsburgh, Pa.
12 Richmond, Va.
13 Wilmington, Del.

Southeast Region
14 Atlanta, Ga.
15 Birmingham, Ala.

16 Chamblee, Ga.
17 Columbia, S.C.
18 Greensboro, N.C.
19 Jackson, Miss.
20 Jacksonville, Fla.
21 Memphis, Tenn.
22 Nashville, Tenn.

Southwest Region
23 Albuquerque, N. Mex.
24 Austin, Tex.
25 Cheyenne, Wyo.
26 Dallas, Tex.
27 Denver, Colo.
28 Little Rock, Ark.
29 New Orleans, La.
30 Oklahoma City, Okla.
31 Wichita, Kans.

Midwest Region
32 Aberdeen, S. Dak.
33 Chicago, Ill.
34 Des Moines, Iowa
35 Fargo, N. Dak.
36 Kansas City, Mo.
37 Milwaukee, Wis.
38 Omaha, Neb.
39 Springfield, Ill.
40 St. Louis, Mo.
41 St. Paul, Minn.

North Atlantic Region
42 Albany, N.Y.
43 Andover, Mass.
44 Augusta, Maine
45 Boston, Mass.
46 Brooklyn, N.Y.
47 Buffalo, N.Y.
48 Burlington, Vt.
49 Hartford, Conn.

50 Holtsville, N.Y. (Brookhaven SC)
51 Manhattan, N.Y.
52 New York, N.Y.
53 Portsmouth, N.H.
54 Providence, R.I.

Western Region
55 Anchorage, Alaska
56 Boise, Idaho
57 Fresno, Calif.
58 Helena, Mont.
59 Honolulu, Hawaii
60 Los Angeles, Calif.
61 Ogden, Utah
62 Phoenix, Ariz.
63 Portland, Ore.
64 Reno, Nev.
65 Salt Lake City, Utah
66 San Francisco, Calif.
67 Seattle, Wash.

complex audits, usually at the taxpayer's home or office. Both revenue agents and tax auditors have the power to issue summonses to compel a taxpayer to present himself and his records at an IRS location for examination. In 1978, the IRS employed an average of 4,617 tax auditors and 13,927 revenue agents. Both groups are generally referred to as "agents" by taxpayers and their representatives.

The Criminal Investigation Division was formerly called the "Intelligence Division." Its new name is more descriptive of this division's function: criminal audits and investigation of tax crimes. This division had an average of 2,779 "special agents" available during 1978. Special agents are not just another type of auditor; they are law enforcement officers with the power of summons and arrest. Basic training for Criminal Investigation agents is held at the Federal Law Enforcement Training Center at Glynco, Georgia.

The Collection Division does just what its name suggests. Its "revenue officers," all 5,924 of them, enforce Internal Revenue's collection policy. They will use whatever means are necessary, including seizing of and selling a taxpayer's property, to collect any monies due the IRS. They have the power to issue liens and levies to enforce tax payment.

Problem Resolution Program

Taxpayers sometimes have problems with the IRS that are not easily handled through regular channels. To handle these, there is a "Problem Resolution Program."

Supervising this program at national level is the "Problem Resolution Officer" who reports directly to the Commissioner's office. This position, according to Internal Revenue, was established "to respond effectively to the needs of taxpayers and to handle complaints or problems of a persistent nature." This program is also intended to handle charges that "IRS employees harass taxpayers or that

due process and the constitutional rights of individuals are violated by the actions" of IRS employees. The Problem Resolution Officer acts as an "ombudsman" or advocate on the taxpayers' behalf. This functionary handles such complaints or problems directly with the appropriate Regional Commissioner.

There is now also a problem resolution officer, or PRO, at district level. District PROs do not interfere with cases that are already being handled by regular examination, appeals or collection units. However, a PRO can help taxpayers who have problems with such IRS departments; serious situations will be referred to the national PRO for resolution. District level PROs also function as traffic directors, referring a taxpayer to a specific person or section to handle his case. Problems of coordination, for example, transferring a taxpayer's records from one IRS district to another, is also something that a PRO may handle more efficiently than other IRS personnel.

Taxpayers may be referred to a problem resolution officer if a problem is unusual or complicated enough to merit his attention. However, taxpayers specifically requesting to talk to a PRO may do so. The IRS instructs that if a PRO is at the same location, a taxpayer be sent directly to his office. Otherwise his name and phone number are to be given to the taxpayer.

While not a total solution to all the problems taxpayers have with Internal Revenue, this program at least gives taxpayers a willing ear within the IRS.

Opinions

Most taxpayers are intimidated by the IRS. When they compare its size and power, its organization and manpower with their own limited resources, there is a definite tendency to feel helpless.

However, Internal Revenue's powers are

not without legal restraints and curbs. It is very difficult for the IRS to send a taxpayer to jail or to confiscate *all* his property. Anything so drastic must be done through the courts, and there are appeals and opportunities to bargain all along the way. Only the most stubborn of taxpayers goes all the way with the IRS.

Above all, knowledge and competent tax advice can help balance the odds more to a taxpayer's favor. Manuals such as this one hopefully can take much of the mystery and fear out of contact with the tax collectors. A good tax lawyer or accountant can coach the taxpayer and soften the impact on his pocketbook.

Remember that Internal Revenue is not likely to send a hundred agents to audit your books. The IRS works through one man or woman at a time, and you know more about your own affairs than they can ever hope to learn.

The Internal Revenue Service may be the world's largest collection agency, but it is outnumbered, if not intimidated by, the taxpayers; there are so many of them. It knows that its resources are inadequate; actually they are stretched to the limit. There is only one IRS employee for every 1,000 taxpayers. Less than 30 percent of Internal Revenue's work force is composed of auditors or revenue agents; the rest are clerks and support staff of one kind or another.

Every year Internal Revenue is faced with more tax returns to process than the year before; each year the percentage of returns audited declines. Trained auditors are in short supply; the best leave to become private tax consultants, to work the other side of the table.

Read on, learn more and feel better.

Limited Contact Audits 4

Most of what the IRS calls audits are handled at district office level. However, regional service centers also have an auditing function. Each has its own examination division, which handles problems that do not justify district office contact with a taxpayer.

To justify the annual plea for more auditors, the Internal Revenue Service does not choose to describe this service center activity as "auditing." To the IRS, an "audit" is a more complete examination of a taxpayer's books and records performed by a district office. The service center process that questions a taxpayer about specific items on his return and assesses additional taxes is called a "limited contact" program.

To be very technical, we could say that *all* tax returns are audited. All tax returns go through the DIF screening process, which is actually a cursory computer audit. But that would just be quibbling. Let us just describe the service center examinations as "limited contact audits," for that is what they are.

Service center auditing activity is limited to mail contact with the taxpayers. This contact is confined to relatively simple and readily identifiable problems that can be resolved easily by mail. While none is pleasant, none is too serious.

Routine Corrections

During a service center's first processing of individual tax returns, the arithmetic on each is checked by computer. In 1978, errors were found on 6.4 percent of the returns checked. When a mistake is found, the necessary corrections are made and the tax refigured. A computer-generated form letter is automatically sent out, either billing for additional taxes or making an adjustment to the refund due the taxpayer.

Not surprisingly, more errors were found that were in taxpayers' favor than in the IRS' favor. About two million taxpayers made a mistake and paid more taxes than required. Their adjustments or refunds averaged $152.04. Another 3.4 million individual returns were corrected and billed for an average additional tax of $234.76.

Here are Internal Revenue's figures summarizing this activity:

Individual Income Tax Returns Mathematically Verified by Computer*

Number verified by computer	83,915,000
Number of returns on which mathematical error detected	5,404,000
Percent of returns with mathematical error	6.4%

Chart continued on next page

Returns with increase:

Number	3,371,000
Amount	$791,363,000
Average amount	$234.76

Returns with decrease:

Number	2,033,000
Amount	$309,155,000
Average amount	$152.04

*figures for 1978

DIF Correspondence Program

Not all DIF-selected returns are sent to a district office for audit. Some are referred to service centers for resolution. These would normally be those containing questionable items that could be cleared up by mail.

The "DIF Correspondence Program" relies largely on questionnaires and form letters. There are specific forms for every sort of problem likely to concern the service center.

Two of the many forms used are reprinted in this chapter. Form 4742 requests a detailed explanation of medical and dental expenses claimed on the tax return; Form 4745 asks for a clarification of interest expenses.

Both—and this is typical—require attachments, such as receipts and cancelled checks, as documentation to substantiate the expenses claimed. Return of any documents submitted is promised, although current forms specify that "photocopies are acceptable."

Unallowable Items

Returns questioned under the DIF Correspondence Program represent only about five percent of the audit workload at a typical regional service center.

Another project, the "Unallowable Items Program" is much larger. Approximately 70 percent of the limited contact audits performed by a service center fall into this category. A complete listing of these items will be found in Appendix 1. Before an office or field audit and before filing your return, this list should be reviewed to see if any items will present problems for you.

In an earlier chapter, the essentials of this program were covered. Here, though, to give a better idea of what the program entails are excerpts from some of the form letters sent to taxpayers with unallowable items on their returns:

Personal or Living Expenses—Medical Care

Your medical expense deduction, reported on Schedule A, has been adjusted because deductions for personal, living, or family expenses are not allowable unless expressly provided for in the law. Expenses for items such as meals and lodging, health club dues, diet foods, funeral expenses, and maternity clothes not furnished by a hospital or similar institution as a necessary incident to medical care, are not provided for and are therefore not deductible.

For details, see publication 502, Deductions for Medical and Dental Expenses, available free from the Internal Revenue Service.

Fractional Exemption

The partial exemption you claimed on your return has been disallowed because the law does not provide for fractional or partial exemptions.

Auto Licenses and Tags

Your deduction for automobile license, registration, tag fees, or taxes reported on Schedule A, has been adjusted. The law provides that such amounts may be deductible as personal property taxes only if they are imposed by your state annually and in an amount based on the value of your automobile. Because your state does not impose the fees and taxes in this manner, they do not qualify as personal property taxes and are therefore not deductible.

Educational Expenses for Others

Your deduction for educational expenses for someone other than yourself or your spouse, reported on Schedule A, has been disallowed. Deductions for personal, living or family expenses are allowable only if expressly provided for, in the law. Educational expenses for someone other than yourself or your spouse are not provided for, and are therefore not deductible.

Protest

A deduction, credit, omission of income, or other adjustment on a Federal tax return as an expression of war or other protest is not provided for in the law. We have corrected your tax for the adjustment you made."

The Importance of Form Letters

Similar form letters or questionnaires are sent to taxpayers whose returns are being questioned under most of the rest of the service center audit programs. This would include such efforts as the "Head of Household" program, and taxpayers reported by the Social Security Administration for having possible unreported income.

Service center computers have a reputation for occasionally generating inappropriate form letters. Under the pressure of a heavy work load and a very complicated system, mistakes are probably inevitable.

In such a case, don't ignore the letter; it probably is the form which most closely fits your problem (there isn't an IRS form for every purpose, no matter how many they have). Don't be a wise guy either, and write an abusive letter back. Just write an explanation on the form where it seems most appropriate. Put a big N/A for "not applicable" in any space or question that doesn't apply to you, sign the form if requested, and return it promptly.

Despite the possibility of error, most letters sent out by the service centers are pertinent and understandable. It is important to pay attention to this computer-generated correspondence. Do not ignore or give less than full attention to what may seem like simple questions on the form. It is almost certain that any questions raised by the service center and its computer are the only ones a taxpayer will confront that year if resolved at this stage, and that an initial decision has already been made not to select the return for a real audit.

If you have previously made a mistake on your return, either mathematical or factual in nature, do not compound the error by filing erroneous answers to the additional questions asked by the service center. If any part of your return was guesswork, now is the time to leave the world of fiction and enter the world of reality.

If the service center examination unit cannot clear up a problem, or if they are not satisfied with what they judge to be fabricated answers, the tax return will undoubtedly be passed along to a district office for more personal contact with the taxpayer. And with such contact always lies the possibility, or even the likelihood, of the audit expanding to cover other questions, perhaps other areas best left unexplored by the IRS.

This is not to say that a taxpayer should cave in when he receives a form letter from a service center. However, he should ask himself whether the computer has uncovered anything significant or is just doing its thing—basically, nitpicking. If other problems may come to light if the return goes to the district office, it may be worth your while to make the computer very happy.

Form **4742** (Rev. Feb. 1978)	**Questionnaire — Medical and Dental Expenses**

Taxpayer(s) Name(s) and Address	In Reply Refer To
	Taxable Year

Please furnish the following information to support the deduction for medical and dental expenses shown on your Federal income tax return for the taxable year identified above. If you need more space, please attach extra sheets and number the items to correspond with those below. Attach documents, such as receipts and canceled checks, to substantiate the expenses *(photocopies are acceptable)*. We will return the documents as soon as we are through with them.

Thank you for your cooperation.

Name and Relationship of Person for Whom Paid	Name and Address of Person to Whom Paid	Amounts Paid		Date Paid	Paid by (Check, Cash, etc.)	Is Receipt or Canceled Check Attached?	
		Drugs and Medicines	Insurance, Doctors' Fees, Hospital Bills, etc.			Yes	No

If any part of the medical expense paid was for any person not claimed as an exemption on your return, please give the name, address, and relationship of that person. Also state whether or not you furnished over one-half of the support of that person.

Reimbursement	Show below what part of your medical expenses reported above has been paid by hospitalization, health, or accident insurance. Indicate "None" if applicable.		
	Kind of Coverage	Amount Paid	Name and Address of Insurance Firm
	Drugs and Medicines		
	Doctor and Dental Fees		
	Hospital Bills		

Form 4742 (Rev. 2-78)   *(Continued on back)*   Department of the Treasury - Internal Revenue Service

1. If nursing services in your home are included as medical expenses, describe each service performed by the nurse, and show the percentage of time applicable to each.

2. If traveling or transportation expenses are included as medical expenses, explain in detail the reason for travel or transportation for each individual involved.

3. If meals and lodging, other than in a hospital, are included as medical expenses, explain in detail the reason these expenses were necessary for each individual, particularly the kind of institution in which the meals or lodging were received and the reason for being there.

4. Does your deduction for insurance premiums provide coverage for the loss of earnings, life, limb, eye, etc., along with reimbursement for medical expenses?

☐ Yes   ☐ No   If yes, show the amount of premiums allocable to reimbursement for medical expenses only. $ _____

5. Describe the evidence you are submitting with this questionnaire, if other than a receipt or a canceled check.

Additional information *(if needed)*.

DECLARATION	Your Signature	Date
I declare that I have examined the information on this form and, to the best of my knowledge and belief, it is true, correct, and complete.	Spouse's Signature, If A Joint Return Was Filed	Date

Form 4742 (Rev. 2-78)   Department of the Treasury - Internal Revenue Service

Form **4745** (Rev. May 1978)	Department of the Treasury - Internal Revenue Service **QUESTIONNAIRE - INTEREST EXPENSES**

Taxpayer's name and address	In reply refer to:
	Tax year

Please furnish us information to support the interest deducted on your Federal income tax return for the above year.

You should complete Part I of this form for contracts that show interest or fully deductible finance charges separately from other finance charges. Some examples of fully deductible finance charges are those added to revolving charge accounts by retail stores if the charges are based on the unpaid balance and figured monthly, and bank credit card plans if no part of the charge is for service charges, loan fees, credit investigations, etc. However, you can send us a statement from the firm or person to whom you paid fully deductible finance charges or interest. In this case, you do not need to complete Part I of this form or send other supporting records.

Complete Part II on the back of this form for contracts that do not show the interest charge separately, or for those that involve finance charges that are not fully deductible.

If you need more space, you may use extra sheets numbered to match the items on this form. You can also get more forms from any Internal Revenue Service office.

If you need to use this form, please complete it and mail it to us with any supporting records such as receipts, contracts, and payment books (photocopies are acceptable). We will return your records as soon as we are finished with them.

Thank you for your cooperation.

PART I

Contracts That Show Interest or Fully Deductible Finance Charges Separately From Other Finance Charges
(Please use a separate column for each contract)

1. Kind of loan *(mortgage, automobile, personal, investment, etc.)*			
2. Name of person or firm paid			
3. Date loan was made			
4. Length of time of loan			
5. Interest rate specified	%	%	%
6. Total amount of loan	$	$	$
7. Amount of each payment	$	$	$
8. Interest paid during above tax year	$	$	$

Form **4745** (Rev. 5-78)

PART II

Contracts That Do Not Show Interest or Fully Deductible Finance Charges Separately
(Please use a separate column for each contract)

9. Item bought				
10. Name of person or firm paid				
11. Total cost of item		$	$	$
12. Total finance charges for life of contract		$	$	$
13. Total number of monthly payments required over period of contract				
14.	January	$	S	$
	February			
	March			
	April			
	May			
Unpaid Balance On First Day of Each Month	June			
	July			
	August			
	September			
	October			
	November			
	December			
15. Total unpaid balances above		$	$	$
16. Average balance *(Divide total of each column of line 15 above by 12)*		$	$	$
17. 6% of amount in each column of line 16 above		$	$	$

DECLARATION	Your signature		Date
I declare that I have examined the information on this form and, to the best of my knowledge and belief, it is true, correct, and complete.	Spouse's signature *(if a joint return was filed)*		Date

Form **4745** (Rev 5-78)

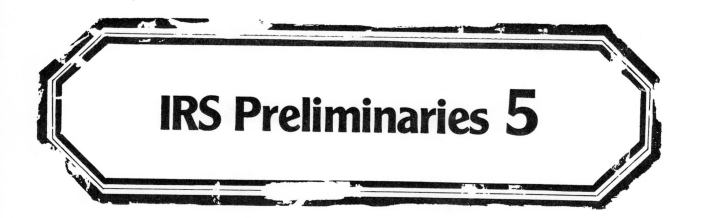

Internal Revenue's selection of tax returns for audit is a multi-stage process. One of the best features of the process is that at each step, additional taxpayers are dropped from further consideration.

As we have seen, all returns are run through the DIF screening process. "High score" returns, those with the greatest potential for a tax increase, are listed on an inventory file to await a possible audit. "Classifiers" pick the most promising of these and review the returns for audit potential. Some are dropped, and the rest assigned to an auditor.

Even at this stage, some returns can still be rejected as not worthy of audit.

Admittedly, once in the hands of the individual who will perform the tax examination, few returns are actually rejected. However, it does happen. To understand why and how, let us review what occurs before the taxpayer is notified of audit.

The Auditor's Preliminaries

The IRS puts a great deal of emphasis on what it calls a "quality audit." According to IRS Manual 4233, a quality audit "is an examination made in a manner reflecting professional efficiency, planning, and direction and pursued to a point where the agent can, with reasonable certainty, conclude that he/she has considered all areas necessary for a proper determination of the tax liability."

To quote again from the manual: "The work of an income tax examiner is professional and should be viewed in that light. Nothing detracts from professional performance as much as lack of preparation for the immediate job at hand."

An audit is obviously not intended to be a hit-or-miss proposition. The IRS, in its training sessions and audit handbooks, stresses preparation and pre-planning. Instructions to agents are specific.

An assigned return comes to the auditor in a "case jacket." If there has been an audit of the particular taxpayer in the past, the previous examiner's "report of examination" is usually included in the jacket. Each auditor prepares a set of "workpapers" that record the findings of his examination step-by-step. If desired, the workpapers on any prior audits may also be requisitioned from the taxpayer's "administrative file."

Depending on the procedures in the particular district, the auditor may also obtain prior years' tax returns that have not been audited and are still "open." This means that returns up to three years old will likely find their way to the examiner's desk.

If the taxpayer whose return is being checked has been over the coals before, the auditor carefully reads the reports of the earlier examination(s). Past workpapers are referred to as necessary. The newly assigned return is checked to see if there are any recurring issues or whether corrective action has been taken on problems uncovered during prior examinations.

Now the audit proper begins, and still the taxpayer has not been notified. The examiner scrutinizes the assigned return, looking for items that merit investigation. He makes notes as he goes on an IRS Form 4315, starting his own set of formal workpapers for this audit.

On an individual short form return (Form 1040A), he may make note of the exemptions claimed to later verify if the children claimed live with the taxpayer. He may also want to check to see if the exemptions are for persons other than children. Excessive refunds may also be noted for later probing.

On itemized returns, the possibilities are greater. Here is a list of items from the IRS "Audit Technique Handbook" that an auditor should verify on a Form 1040 "nonbusiness" return. Naturally, not all of these will be found on a single return.

" (a) Disproportionate or inadequately explained deductions and exclusions from gross income. (Sick pay exclusion, for example.)

(b) Use of income averaging formula.

(c) Unexplained or apparent unreasonable deductions from gross rent or royalties.

(d) Capital gain and loss schedules indicating capital gain treatment for noncapital assets; sales for nominal consideration; use of capital loss carryovers; installment reporting of gains; and problems of 'unstated interest' in installment sales.

(e) Gains and losses from other than capital assets including use of IRC 1231; and discounts on obligations of the buyer.

(f) Disproportionate amount of income vs. number of exemptions claimed.

(g) Casualty losses inadequately explained as to method of loss determination.

(h) Deductions for dependents outside immediate family or living apart from taxpayer.

(i) Excessive refunds.

(j) Inadequate or incomplete schedules or responses to questions on return.

(k) Required schedules not furnished, such as: multiple support agreement and Schedule F (Form 1040).

(l) Business vs. nonbusiness treatment of bad debt losses claimed.

(m) Separate filing by spouse indicated.

(n) Employee's moving expenses.

(o) Recovered amounts deducted in prior years, such as bad debts, medical expenses, state income and other taxes, losses, etc. must be included in income in the year of recovery."

There are separate lists of verification items for 1040 business returns with a Schedule C (trade or business) or F (farm) and for partnership returns.

Any other documents in the case jacket are then considered. There may be a Form 918A, a "Notice of Examination of Fiduciary, Partnership, or Small Business Corporation Return." This advises the auditor that another IRS office is auditing a return in which the taxpayer has an interest. In this case, examination of the assigned return is usually deferred until the results of the first audit are available.

An informer's letter may be in the jacket. A comparison of the allegations in the letter is made with the information on the return. This will usually add an item or two to the workpaper list of specifics to be looked into.

By now, if he is working on the return of a taxpayer with a complicated or unusual business life, the auditor may have run into some problems. The income tax law is so complex that even the IRS does not expect its examiners to be familiar with all of its ramifications. The agent may have to do some research, to check the specifics of the tax law and IRS regulations, to study Treasury decisions, IRS rulings, court cases and other sources that bear on the tax return before him.

After having reviewed the return and any supporting documents, started his workpapers, and undertaken his research, the auditor may still decide that the return is unworthy of examination. Some few taxpayers become lucky at this point when the examiner makes a decision to "survey" the file and drop it from his inventory.

More than a sense of fairness is operating here. Auditors work under an informal system of quotas; his time must produce results in the form of additional assessments. Too many cases that result in the assessment of little or no additional taxes reflect upon the auditor's judgment, with a probable effect on his promotion prospects. To be normal in the IRS bureaucracy is to be cautious, and this can sometimes work to a taxpayer's advantage.

Once a decision is made to retain the case jacket in inventory, the taxpayer will be notified at some point that an examination of his tax return is being conducted.

Notification of an Audit

The actual notice to the taxpayer that his return is being audited may take one of several different forms, depending on the type of audit.

After a classifier has reviewed and selected returns for audit, they are routed to either a tax auditor or to a revenue agent for follow-up. A tax auditor works in a district office or in one of its branches, and conducts what might best be described as a "desk audit." They are given the simpler questions to resolve and usually spend no more than two or three hours on each taxpayer's return.

A revenue agent is more experienced, with a higher level of accounting education. More complex returns are assigned this type of agent for investigation for a "field audit," which normally is conducted at the taxpayer's place of business or his home. Audits by revenue agents may take one or two or even more working days to complete.

To notify a taxpayer of an audit tax auditors utilize a form letter. Usually prepared en masse by the clerical staff in the IRS office the bad news will start something like this:

"We are examining your Federal income tax return for the above year(s) and find we need additional information to verify your correct tax. We have, therefore, scheduled the above appointment for you. . . ."

A specific date and time tell the taxpayer when to appear; the address of the IRS office tells him where to appear. The taxpayer is also informed that he may be accompanied or represented by his tax advisor. Because office audits are usually limited to a few questionable items, the invitation will also describe what records must be brought for inspection.

When you do go to the IRS office, bring the records requested and anything else you think you might need to win your case on the items questioned—but nothing else. If the conference turns to additional items, matters for which you are not prepared, politely decline to discuss them until you review your records. *Do not ad lib.*

A revenue agent's initial approach to a taxpayer follows one of two patterns, depending upon the type of office that he works out of.

In a large metropolitan area where the IRS office is located relatively near the taxpayer, the revenue agent is likely just to phone the taxpayer. The manual specifically instructs the agent to call the taxpayer, not his representative, though a referral to a tax representative by the taxpayer will generally be accepted by the agent. On this initial contact, the agent will notify the taxpayer of the audit and attempt to set an appointment.

Letters are used only when it is impractical or impossible to contact the taxpayer by phone. Such a situation might arise with an individual who works away from his home base, or with someone who has no phone.

If a referral to a taxpayer's representative "unreasonably" delays or "hinders the examination," the agent will request permission from his group manager to proceed with the taxpayer directly.

Though the manual instructs revenue agents to make their initial contact and to work out an appointment by phone or by mail, in real life such is not always the case. Many agents will just "drop by" a business and try for an immediate audit. This would indicate either poor time planning by the agent or an attempt to catch a taxpayer by surprise. You should assume the latter. If his drop-in call is inconvenient, tell him so, and ask him to return when you have organized your records and can tend to the audit in a businesslike manner.

In an IRS office covering a more thinly-populated area, phone calls are not used as much, largely to hold down the phone bills. Where travel is involved, agents are instructed to preplan and to group their audits by geographical area. Appointments are made by mail, well in advance, to allow for any necessary schedule adjustments. Moreover, traveling agents are instructed to carry a supply of "reserve" cases. These are used to fill in whenever there is unforeseen idle time. The unlucky (because perhaps they would not have been audited otherwise) "reserve" taxpayers are contacted by local phone to arrange an audit. Because of this practice of carrying backup cases, taxpayers in small towns and rural areas are more subject to "short notice" audits than those in big cities.

This chapter has been devoted largely to explaining how an auditor prepares for the examination of a tax return. The main reason is to give the reader an idea of what he is up against. But more important, because it will help the taxpayer to maintain some control over the audit, is the taxpayer's own preparation.

The Taxpayer's Preparation 6

The frame of mind of a taxpayer getting himself ready for an audit should ideally be one of quiet confidence. This does not mean he should expect his return to be accepted, as filed, by the agent. Total satisfaction of the agent with the return may, in fact, indicate weakness, not strength; the taxpayer is probably paying too much.

Instead, this quiet confidence involves a number of things: peace of mind that the return is *arguably* correct; that *available* records or testimony are adequate to support the taxpayer's position as reflected on the return; and that such records or the individuals whose testimony is needed will be ready for the audit.

A taxpayer should accept the fact that tax audits, while relatively rare in terms of percentages, are a way of life in our self-assessment system. He should also understand that a "no-change" return (one that does not result in a change in tax liability upon audit) may indicate less than an aggressive, hard-nosed approach to preparing the return in the first place—and not perfection or even good citizenship.

In its annual attempts to justify additional agents in its budget, the IRS presents its statistics in such a way as to obscure the true picture of voluntary compliance among the taxpaying public. Actually, IRS figures for "no-change" returns reveal a very low rate of voluntary acceptance of the IRS' position on a number of tax questions. In 1976, the General Accounting Office discovered and reported that the voluntary compliance rate, which the IRS uses to demonstrate how well the tax system works, is much higher than the "no-change" rate, which indicates the number of taxpayers who report their tax liability correctly.

The Professional Advantage

In any field, the professional has the advantage of greater experience. Each transaction adds an incremental bit of know how that increases his edge for the next go-around. You may buy a refrigerator once every 10 years or so; an appliance salesman might sell three a day, 1,000 in a year, 10,000 in 10 years.

So it is with tax audits. On your first or second audit, you may go up against an agent with thousands of examinations under his belt. Even a young and relatively green auditor with six months' experience might have completed 200 audits by the time he gets your case jacket on his desk.

Obviously, it behooves a taxpayer to do what he can to even the odds a bit. If you are reading this you are already taking an important first step—educating yourself on the audit process. Your objective should be to learn enough to take the weapon of surprise away from the auditor.

The second step is to review your return, gather whatever supporting evidence is necessary, and put it in order. Third, and maybe the most important, is to hire yourself some professional support.

Reviewing Your Return

A review is mandatory self-defense. By the time the IRS informs you that your tax return is to be examined, your memory of its specifics will generally have faded. Months, perhaps a year or more, will have gone by since the forms were completed and mailed.

Audit notification letters from a tax auditor will list the particular areas the examiner will check. Field audits are much more general than desk audits; a phone call from a revenue agent will require a more extensive review on your part.

The goal in a field audit is more than just to refresh your memory. Your copy of the return and any subsidiary schedules should be studied with an eye for what the IRS might be interested in. Is income understated? Are exemptions real and justifiable? Are claimed deductions reasonable and within normal limits? Are there any weak spots that you would prefer not to be questioned about? Does your return include anything from the list earlier in this chapter of items an auditor is expected to verify?

If your return was prepared with professional help, you should contact the tax preparer and arrange to have him review the return with you, even if you do not want him to accompany you to the conference. If you do not consider the preparer an expert in terms of his own experience with tax law and audits, find one just for the purpose of preparing you for the audit.

A knowledgeable professional can help, both with the routine and the unusual. He will generally be aware of any areas to which the local IRS office is giving special emphasis. Perhaps they are looking carefully into home office deductions, and auditing all antique

dealers looking for unreported cash income. If you are an antique dealer with a home office, such information can border on the critical.

Sometimes a fresh look by a real professional will turn a problem into a solution. For example, suppose your preparer claimed a loan to an acquaintance as a business bad debt when it was not repaid. The IRS could make the disallowance of an ordinary deduction stick. But a creative professional might develop a new legal theory to support the same deduction, such as the fact that the borrower had induced the loan by misrepresenting his poor financial condition. Under state law, this would constitute "larceny-by-trick," and the loan would become an allowable casualty (theft) loss.

A second opinion is as important in the area of taxes as it is in medicine.

Supporting Evidence

Gathering supporting evidence is also a necessary preliminary. An unpleasant truth of the audit system is that the burden of proof is on the taxpayer. When a return is completed, deductions can be claimed for any amount without proof. The odds are against any tax deductions ever being questioned. That is, until audit time, when the odds swing the other way.

An extreme example of the need for supporting evidence is the whole area of business entertainment. Until 1963, businessmen were allowed to estimate when they took deductions for entertainment expenses. The only limits were those of reasonableness; detailed records were unnecessary. Besides, after a good meal and a few drinks with a customer or client, who ever wrote anything down anyway?

In 1963, the rules were revised and tightened. Now a taxpayer must write it down and, preferably, get a receipt. Diaries, notes on who and where and why, and receipts for amounts over $25 are all required. Reasonableness now counts for nothing; the general rule now is no proof, no deduction.

What constitutes proof? Good documentation is a record generated by a third party, a cash receipt, an invoice marked "paid." A taxpayer's unsupported cancelled check is often suspect to an auditor; a check made out to "Dr. Jones" might be payment for a used set of golf clubs and not proof of a legitimate medical expense. Matching documents are the best evidence—an invoice, together with the cancelled check paying that particular bill.

The Time Element

To review your return, consult with a tax professional, and gather the necessary supporting evidence takes time. You must make certain that the auditor allows you enough time to prepare for an examination. Usually, a letter requesting the pleasure of your presence at an IRS location for an office audit will present no problem. A month's, or at least a couple of weeks', advance warning is normally given. Nevertheless, if your work schedule or that of your representative conflicts with the appointment date, do not hesitate to reschedule. In fact, a postponement to put your records in shape is preferable to appearing with a bag of papers and notes. But under no circumstances should you fail to appear without calling at least a day or two in advance, if possible. Just pick up the phone and call the number given. Letters from large IRS offices will sometimes give the name of a special appointments clerk.

A phone call from a revenue agent is more informal, but more is involved in the way of preparation and more is at stake. A field audit will take more time than the more limited examinations held in an IRS office. The same principles apply. Schedule only at your convenience; allow yourself enough time for an adequate review and consultation and to collect your supporting records—and your wits.

There is no substitute for orderliness. Retaining and organizing supporting documents and presenting them during an audit in an efficient way can be the difference between an examination lasting an hour or two and years of bureaucratic hassle.

If substantial correspondence or other documentation is needed to justify a deduction, sort the documents into chronological or some other sensible order. Consider placing them in a series of file folders, or even in plastic sleeves in a looseleaf binder. If checks are involved, cull the needed ones from your bank statements. Take along only those checks that pertain to the questions under review; don't bring all your cancelled checks and tempt the agent to riffle through them all.

An agent appearing at your door, trying for an immediate audit, is out of line. Although he may be acting with the knowledge of his immediate superiors (and he also may not be), the agent is acting contrary to the guidelines laid down in the IRS audit manuals. You are within your rights if you insist upon sufficient time to prepare. Even one or two days' notice, though better than an immediate audit, does not provide enough warning.

Professional Help

From the scattered references so far for using a tax professional to help you to prepare for audit, you have probably surmised the basic idea. If the tax law is too complex for the IRS to expect its auditors to understand completely, it is definitely too complex for the average taxpayer. If the examination of tax returns is professional work, then the taxpayer had better hire his own professional. The simple truth is that unless your income is quite low and from salary only, your affairs uncomplicated, and your return unitemized, you probably need help in dealing with an audit.

Another basic truth is that you probably can't afford not to use a tax professional. The object of an audit is to squeeze your pocketbook, to wring out more tax dollars. In 1978, the average "recommendation" for additional taxes on the simpler, less complex returns examined by tax auditors was $322. For field audits by revenue agents, the average extra assessment was $3,898. Unless your filing was so miserably prepared as to be beyond salvage, any competent tax professional should be able to help hold down an assessment enough to justify his fee.

Who is a "tax professional"? Generally, he is an accountant or lawyer. Taxes are a field involving both law and accountancy; the professions overlap. At the top end, and most expensive, are combination CPA-lawyers, potent specialists in short supply. Many lawyers also specialize in taxes. It is to a taxpayer's definite advantage, *if there are any potential criminal problems involved,* to have a lawyer represent him before the IRS. Such sensitive spots might include tax fraud, tax evasion, conspiracy of many varieties, and willful failure to file or to pay taxes. In such areas, the attorney-client privilege becomes important.

For most taxpayers, where the controversy with the IRS involves mainly the amount of taxes due, CPAs specializing in taxes, general practitioner CPAs, and public accountants are more than sufficient. Non-CPA accountants must be "enrolled" to practice before the IRS, first passing an extensive examination on tax procedures and law.

Non-accountant tax preparers, who work perhaps three months a year preparing simpler returns for wage earners, are normally not adequate assistance at audit time. For one thing, they are not usually available 12 months a year; they tend to fade away into other lines of work after April 15. As non-professionals, they are also unlikely to be qualified to represent a taxpayer before the IRS at an audit or appeal.

Costs for professional help will run from perhaps $20 an hour for a general-practice accountant to over $50 an hour for a CPA-tax specialist. Combination CPA-lawyers are rarer birds and expensive, at $100 an hour or more. They are probably needed only by corporations and other high-rollers facing potentially serious trouble with the IRS.

Should a tax advisor just hold a taxpayer's hand, or do it all? There is a school of thought that advocates a taxpayer having little or no contact with the IRS. The reasoning goes that a layman, face-to-face with an aggressive auditor, is likely to reveal too much. Most people are much too cooperative in the face of authority. A taxpayer is likely to talk too much, to over-answer questions, to lead the auditor into areas best left unexplored, and to agree too readily with the auditor's proposed assessments. There is also the reverse danger, that a taxpayer will be uncooperative, perhaps even lie when asked leading questions. Lying to an IRS agent can open up a whole new can of troubles. False statements to the IRS can be perjury, punishable under the Internal Revenue Code by fines up to $5,000 and imprisonment for up to three years.

The reasoning continues that a tax professional, acting in a taxpayer's stead as his representative, is likely to steer the middle course. He is unlikely to be intimidated by an auditor, and equally unlikely to violate any of the provisions of the law that can escalate a relatively minor civil audit into a major one, or even into a criminal case.

Other tax professionals believe that, at least in comparatively simple matters, advance consultation with an advisor is enough; they feel the very appearance of a professional may give an auditor reason to think he is onto something. After consultation, so goes this theory, the taxpayer should be able to handle a conference with the auditor on his own, with the professional waiting in the wings in case trouble develops requiring further encounters.

A compromise school of thought, and perhaps the most practical, is that basically the advisor should handle all contact with the IRS, but the taxpayer may come along to answer specific questions. If the client-taxpayer has little or nothing to hide involving the issues raised, particularly where a simple office audit is involved, he can accompany his hired gun to the IRS office. The advisor handles all explanations and negotiations; the taxpayer basically keeps his mouth shut, observes all, and answers (always truthfully) only those questions his advisor asks him, in the manner rehearsed in advance.

Another great advantage to using a tax representative is that a field audit can be held on the representative's premises. The IRS "Audit Technique Handbook" instructs agents to "attempt to dissuade the taxpayer from such practice." Internal Revenue would rather hold an audit at a taxpayer's place of business or his home. They will resist the idea of working at a law or accounting office, with less than total access to the taxpayer's records. However, there is no law allowing the IRS to force the issue at this stage. If the taxpayer and his representative agree, they should insist that the audit be held at a place of their choosing.

Selecting a Tax Advisor

If you do not have a tax advisor, perhaps the best place to start is by asking around your circle of business acquaintances. Try your banker, your insurance agent, or someone you know who has recently been audited. If possible, try to come up with two or three recommendations. Then phone and ask for an appointment with each. Discuss fees, the services they provide, and try to get an idea of their philosophy towards the IRS (this can range from total submission to aggressive avoidance) before making a decision.

The best time to do this, if possible, is before you get a notice of audit and when they are not in the midst of a hectic "tax season." Professionals accept, though, that most new clients will come to them because of tax troubles, and that usually means a pending audit.

Internal Revenue requires that the taxpayer sign a power-of-attorney, authorizing a particular accountant or lawyer to represent him in tax matters. This is routine; the advisor will have the necessary forms.

For more information on choosing a tax advisor, you may want to read the May 1979 issue of *Tax Angles* which contains an excellent article on the subject ($3 from *Tax Angles*, 901 North Washington St., Alexandria, VA 22314).

The Audit Itself 7

Two types of tax audits are conducted at the district office level, "office" audits and the more extensive "field" audits.

Office Audits

This category of examination is a step up from the "limited contact audits" performed by a regional service center. Questionnaires are used by a service center to obtain information to verify a specific deduction or claim on a taxpayer's return. But there is a point at which a mail audit becomes impractical.

Most commonly, several important issues or areas of a return need to be reviewed. Sometimes the amount of documentation an auditor would like to see would be inconvenient to handle by mail; more often, the documents may not adequately describe a transaction. Explanations by the taxpayer or his representative may be needed. Perhaps the auditor wants to judge the taxpayer's credibility. Maybe there were indications on a return that a taxpayer would be unable to complete a questionnaire satisfactorily, or problems of illiteracy requiring verbal contact. (The IRS has some forms in Spanish, Chinese and Vietnamese, but if an audit were attempted on a taxpayer who used one, an interpreter would undoubtedly be needed.) And then again, the service center may have tried to piece together a transaction and failed, and the return ends up in a district office for resolution.

All this is grist for a tax auditor in an IRS district office. About 75 percent of all the returns audited at district office level, and over 80 percent of the individual returns are handled as office audits.

Generally, an office audit can be expected to take at least an hour, and often much longer. Up to a point, it is to the taxpayer's advantage to have the entire process run as quickly and efficiently as possible. And this is where preparation helps. If a taxpayer has reviewed the return in question, gathered and organized his records bearing on the likely issues, supporting documents can be produced without delay.

This helps keep the examiner's attention on the item in question. If a taxpayer's records are in disarray, and it takes time to dig through the mess to find a receipt or whatever, there is a danger of expanding the audit. While waiting, the auditor's attention might be caught by another potentially interesting item. Never give the auditor time to ponder or to speculate on the possibility for further assessments. Do not expose him to more of your records and life than you have to.

Sometimes, under pressures of a heavy schedule, an auditor might be anxious to press on to the next case. If two or three issues are resolved in a taxpayer's favor because of business-like preparation and adequate proof, the auditor might decide to finish the examination quickly. Any remaining questions might be skipped over as probably not worth the additional time.

To encourage such an attitude a taxpayer should appear cooperative and yet be quiet and calm, certainly not talkative. Be polite and businesslike. Answer questions as minimally as possible, volunteer nothing, and provide just the records requested.

Other general rules are to be on time, don't express anger or dissatisfaction with the government or the IRS, never blame the auditor personally for the state of the nation, and smile once in awhile.

You may feel like a hypocrite, but these are only universal rules for dealing with a powerful bureaucracy. A taxpayer may find a strong approach effective with his town water board, but they do not have the power to disrupt his life that the IRS does. At an audit in an IRS office, the general rule to keep in mind is: "the quicker the audit, the happier the auditor, and the less likelihood of opening up new areas of the return for consideration." (While the IRS has repeatedly denied that agents have quotas, they are promoted on the basis of performance, which breaks down into returns audited, time spent, and new taxes assessed.)

Cooperation only goes so far, though. Internal Revenue's objective in any audit is always to etablish a deficiency, to generate some more tax revenue. If it costs you too much money, you have to take steps to defend yourself.

Though an office audit is less complex, with fewer issues examined than a field audit, employing a tax representative is still a good idea. Tax auditors are often unseasoned and tax regulations are full of gray areas. A deduction at issue might be decided either way. Up against only a layman, an auditor is likely to decide the issue his way. With an experienced tax professional present on the side of the

taxpayer, the game changes. An agent is less likely to push, is forced to be more objective, to take less and concede more.

Another advantage of having a professional present or being represented by one at an office audit, is that an informal appeal from an auditor's decision can be made immediately. There is a formal appeals system, both within the IRS and using the courts, that is described later in this manual. What we are talking about now is not a formal appeal but something worth trying sometimes.

If the tax auditor seems antagonistic or unfair or arrives at what seems to be an exaggerated new assessment, the matter should be discussed with his immediate superior *before the audit is formally closed*. There is an important element of timing and approach here. The matter must be taken to the supervisor after all the issues have been examined and a proposed assessment discussed. Any action should be taken before the argument develops to the point where the auditor hardens his position in concrete.

A professional tax representative approaching the auditor's supervisor is likely to be listened to more carefully than an excited taxpayer might be. Again, this is a case of professionals working together to resolve a problem. With luck, the supervisor might agree with you, perhaps out of fairness or merely to exercise his authority over an obstreperous auditor.

To obtain a concession, it might be necessary to agree to an assessment and to pay immediately rather than postponing the matter. (Aspects of closing an audit and payment are covered in other chapters.) Such an agreement on the taxpayer's part can work to reduce both the possible assessment and the potential expenses associated with a formal appeal.

You should remember that a tax representative's fees become an allowable deduction on next year's tax return. Thus, if you are near the 50 percent tax bracket, a $500 fee to a tax professional would be fully recovered if he were able to reduce your potential tax assessment by only $250.

Field Audits

About 20 to 25 percent of the audits performed by district offices are field audits handled by revenue agents. A revenue agent may have a desk in the local IRS office, but he generally works outside, performing his examinations at taxpayers' homes or business locations. That is, unless a taxpayer knows his rights and insists the audit be conducted at his accountant's or lawyer's work place.

The first rule in dealing with a revenue agent is to be certain that he is indeed a revenue agent. Ask to see his identification, and take enough time to inspect it carefully. Be especially wary if two agents arrive to inspect your books. Demand the identification of both. The second visitor, introduced as "Agent Jones" might well be "Special Agent Jones" from the Criminal Investigation Division. Special agents have been known to stay in the background, keeping a low profile, and letting their companion revenue agent do all the talking and identification-card-showing. Hopefully, if two agents show up at your door, one will just be a trainee and the other a more senior revenue agent giving some on-the-job training.

If you do identify a special agent, politely terminate the interview immediately. It really should not have even started, because checking an agent's ID is the first order of business. The presence of a special agent means that you are under investigation for possible criminal tax charges, a much more serious matter than a routine civil audit. Do not let the special agent examine your records at this time and do not engage in conversation, seemingly casual or not. Anything you say can be used against you, or to develop further leads, even if the agent never gets around to explaining your

rights to you. Use your right to counsel and call your tax advisor immediately; you're going to need all the help you can get.

Normally, field audits do not start off so dramatically. Two chapters from now, special agents and criminal audits will be discussed in more detail.

It is necessary, in fact it is required by the law, that in a civil situation (not a criminal audit) you allow the IRS access to your records for the purposes of verifying your tax self-assessment. (The exact opposite is true in a criminal investigation.) However, it is sensible, self-preservation really, even in a civil audit to control that access to the bare minimum needed to permit the auditor to conduct the audit. Holding the audit at your attorney's or accountant's working quarters usually goes a long way toward accomplishing this goal.

To carry this one step further, it is often desirable to absent yourself entirely and let the tax advisor deal with the agent. Your stated attitude should be, "There is only a legal question involved," or "My accountant knows more about this than I do, anyway!"

Workpapers

In the previous chapter, we described how an auditor starts a set of audit workpapers before contacting the taxpayer. These workpapers follow a standard format prescribed by the IRS. "Worksheet A" is the agent's preliminary analysis of the tax return, his list of items to check further. "Worksheet B" is headed "Discussions" and is a record of his first talk with the taxpayer. But the title is misleading; this worksheet actually covers the taxpayer's living standards and financial history.

Please turn to Appendix 2 at the rear of this manual. A full set of sample worksheets for an individual nonbusiness return is provided as an example. They are reproduced directly from IRS Manual 4233, "Tax Audit Guidelines." You might browse through the worksheets to get an idea of how methodically an auditor approaches a relatively simple audit.

You might as well glance at Appendix 3 at the same time. IRS Audit Guidelines are of two broad types. Some are general and are applicable to all sorts of returns filed by individuals and businesses. Other guidelines are more specialized and describe in detail the problems encountered in examining particular trades, uncommon types of business arrangements, and other special situations. Appendix 3 demonstrates how the IRS codifies its accumulated experience and passes it along to its agents. To retain the flavor of the material, this entire section, guidelines for auditing professional persons, is reproduced directly from IRS Manual 4231. If you are a doctor, dentist, lawyer, architect, funeral director, or the like, this information should be of particular interest.

After having read the material in the two appendices, you will have a better idea of why it is safer for a taxpayer undergoing an audit to limit his personal contact with the agent. Using a representative as a go-between helps restrict the violation of personal financial privacy. Remember, what the agent doesn't know won't hurt you.

Going it Alone

While the arguments in favor of using a professional to accompany you during all contacts with the IRS are persuasive, there is a case to be made against such a practice. One consideration is that the agent may become suspicious, be alerted to dimensions of a problem that might otherwise go unnoticed. An auditor might feel, "If his is such an open-and-shut case, then how come this expensive lawyer is sitting across the table from me?" Perhaps sometimes only the taxpayer should attend a conference—and sometimes only his advisor. The impact of your both being there should be considered.

If, for whatever reasons, you decide to handle the audit contact yourself, there are some basic ground rules to consider. All of the guidelines for taxpayer behavior given for office audits apply for field audits too. Be polite and businesslike when you greet the auditor. Avoid an antagonistic manner; the agent might respond in kind. Don't discuss the federal government's misuse of tax money; the agent will only be irritated even if he personally agrees with you. Above all, avoid any mention of tax rebellion; you might be reported to Criminal Investigation's special "Tax Protestor Project." If you consider taxation to be theft by the government, don't express your views to the agent; by implication you label him a thief too. Unless he's very young and naive, the agent knows how taxpayers feel about him; don't rub it in.

Isolating the Auditor

Since a field audit involves quite a bit of paper-shuffling, the revenue agent will need a place to work. The ideal solution would be to provide him with a table and a chair in a plain room. There should be enough light to work by, and the work space should be comfortable, but should be stripped of all possible restrictions. Tax firms who are routinely hosts to auditors, often have special rooms set aside that are remarkably similar to our ideal. It may be impossible to manage the ideal on your premises, but you should try for a reasonable facsimile.

If the audit is being held in your home (which, if possible, should be avoided), it might be a good idea to send the spouse, and most certainly the children, out for the duration.

If the audit is held at your office, your employees should be instructed to avoid any discussions with the agent. Be careful, though, not to give your employees the idea that you have anything to hide. Certinly no casual socializing should be permitted. If possible, whatever workspace you assign the auditor should be isolated from the normal workflow where the auditor will be unable to hear or see what goes on in the office. Contact should be limited to one person who will be responsible for providing whatever documents are needed.

It may also be a good idea not to schedule sensitive or important meetings while the auditor is working on the premises.

If the field audit is held at a business location, the auditor may request a tour of the premises. A tour provides fodder for yet another worksheet. If not requested, a tour should not be given unless it will clearly help you. Whoever conducts the auditor around should not provide the sort of guided tour given a new employee. Introductions are not to be made except to the treasurer, comptroller, bookkeeping or accounting person who will be the auditor's contact, and perhaps to your secretary who will know where to find you, if needed. Explanations should be simple: "This is our warehouse," "this is our order department," and so on.

If there are unusual items on your tax return that pertain to the physical plant, it might be a good idea to point out the feature. For example, if a casualty deduction was claimed because a section of your facility was flooded or damaged by fire, consider showing the area to the agent, if that will help. If a tax credit was claimed for a significant capital expenditure, include the result of the investment on the tour.

The Time Element

Field audits take time, at least most of a working day and often much longer. Two or three days is not uncommon for a moderately involved business return. The process is often complicated by other demands upon the revenue agent. At the peak of the tax season, for example, audits are sometimes interrupted when agents are called back to the office to help handle the crowds seeking advice. If an examination takes longer than anticipated, after the first session the auditor might not be able to return for a few days because of other scheduled audits. He may work a full day, then come back for a few hours two or three times as the opportunity presents itself.

You are entitled to some effort on his part to expedite the process. You should not hesitate to call the auditor's supervisor if the delay in winding up the audit appears unreasonable and is the fault of the IRS rather than yours. Also, if the agent says he is finished and then attempts to return, you have a statutory right to challenge him upon reappearance.

If, without saying he is through, the auditor returns with a second agent, be sure to check the identification of his companion, just as you would have on the first visit. The second time around it is more likely to be a special agent than a trainee. If it is a "special," freeze everything; go no further and say nothing whatsoever until you have consulted with your tax attorney. If you do not have one, get one—not just an attorney, but one qualified and experienced in tax matters, preferably in criminal tax matters.

Always bear in mind that an agent has one thing in common with you—the desire for a "quick audit." It is in your interest to help him achieve his goal of finishing as quickly as possible. Anything you can do to keep his nose down and busily at work is legitimate. Preorganization, the ability to provide requested supporting paper quickly, helps. So does normal courtesy, at least to the extent of providing access to a restroom, and coffee or water. You and your employees should avoid long discussions about sports or politics with an auditor. An attractive secretary or bookkeeper might be cautioned not to create or pursue conversational openings.

Providing coffee to keep an agent alert and on the job does not mean you should invite him to lunch. An auditor does not expect any special treatment. In fact, he can lose his job by accepting a meal from a taxpayer. Even if you draw an attractive female revenue agent, resist the temptation to tender an invitation. The proper course at lunch time is always to announce the expected time of your return and just leave, inquiring, whenever appropriate, how much more time the agent contemplates the audit will take. (Try to hold him to his estimate, if you can.)

Spot Checking

One of the common ways that an auditor uses to work through his verification list is by running "test checks," sampling the substantiating documents. Take, as an example, travel and entertainment expenses, a deduction found on both business and nonbusiness returns. This is a category of deduction where proof is a must and estimates are not acceptable.

The auditor will choose one or two periods during the taxable year, amounting to perhaps five or 10 items out of a possible 100. Each of the items in the sample will be carefully checked to establish the relationship of the T&E expense to the taxpayer's business, the place of the expenditure, the amount and the identity of the persons involved including those entertained. The auditor will then try to determine if any of these expenditures are of a personal and nonbusiness nature. Always suspect are expenses involving company-owned cars, boats, planes, hunting lodges, hotel suites, trips to resort areas and similar expenses. On nonbusiness returns, another critical question is whether the taxpayer was reimbursed for the expenses by his employer.

If the randomly selected items all pass the tests and are accepted as legitimate, so probably will the remainder. The agent will move on to other areas of interest, happy to have saved some time.

If some of the test items fail and are disallowed, the items unsampled become suspect.

Another sample will be worked; if there are any failures in this test, further probing is called for. This can be narrow, limited perhaps to the company cars or boat, or to convention visits. Or it can be wide, including every T&E expenditure. In any case, the agent has discovered a lode, an area likely to yield a substantial tax deficiency for him.

On an individual nonbusiness return, such a sampling process might also be used for medical expenses or contributions.

Admit Nothing

Whenever a claimed deduction is disallowed, it is a disappointment and is going to cost you money. A revenue agent's goal is to find unreported income, deductions to disallow, credits to challenge, and to add to the tax bill when he does.

The taxpayer's goal is to maximize deductions and to minimize taxes. This is expected. Internal Revenue even expects taxpayers to stretch the truth, the facts, and the law; that's why there are audits and auditors in the first place.

Never assume that an agent is always correct. If he makes comments as he proceeds, take notes. Nod that you understand if you do; ask questions if you don't. Explain that you want to check out everything which seems at least arguable; there is no point in indicating agreement or conceding an issue at this point in an audit. By making concessions during an audit, you will only encourage the agent to push harder.

If you are caught exaggerating or bending the rules some but not too much, most revenue agents don't care. You have only given them an opportunity to pick up some extra tax money which they want to justify their job. But some agents uncovering this sort of thing, will threaten criminal prosecution. Such a course of action is highly improper; it is not an agent's job to threaten or lecture a taxpayer. If an agent threatens you with criminal prosecution: stay cool and respond courteously, either giving a reasonable explanation for your inaccuracy or mistake, or saying nothing.

Some taxpayers have been known to compound the consequences beyond a mere tax deficiency. Don't ever volunteer a confession; the agent is not a priest. There is no reason to confess to "criminal" intent. Never admit you knew what you were doing if you deducted your wife's travel expenses when she vacationed in Hawaii when you went there on a sales trip, or when you claimed veterinary fees for your cat as part of your medical expenses. Never, never say anything like, "I might have known you'd catch me."

If you feel the need to say anything, let it be, "I didn't know that." Better yet is, "I want to check out the law on that," or even, "I don't agree with you, but I want to get this over with." Even silence beats a confession. It is more sensible to seem stupid than to confess to what an agent could characterize as "willful tax evasion."

In most cases, the agent will like it better too. He really doesn't want to report you to Criminal Investigation for a tax fraud investigation just because you admitted to him that you knowingly tried to defraud the government of taxes. He'd rather just disallow your deduction, add to your assessment, and leave it at that.

Statute of Limitations

Generally, Internal Revenue has only three years to audit a tax return and to make any additional assessments. Barring fraud or a substantial understatement of your gross income, any taxes not assessed within this period are lost forever. This time runs from the filing date, or the date on which the return became due, whichever comes later. For example, on a return filed on March 10, 1981 but due April 15, 1981, the IRS has until April 15, 1984, three years after the due date, to complete its audit, propose a deficiency, and make an assessment.

This is not an ironclad rule, though. These basic limitations do not apply for fraudulent returns, returns with income understated by 25 percent or more, or in cases where no return was filed. Proof of fraud can extend the statute of limitations for civil purposes indefinitely; for criminal cases, six years is the rule. A 25 percent omission of gross income on your return, even if not proven fraudulent, will extend the statutory limit to six years.

While negligence is no excuse, full disclosure is . If the choice when filing your return comes to disclosing and deducting or omitting income, do the former. As an example, full disclosure of a payment from a close relative which is thought to be exempt as a gift, will not extend the limits, even if the taxpayer is wrong. (Both the amount and its nature must be disclosed.)

The statute of limitations will also not apply if the taxpayer signs a waiver, a "Consent to Extend the Time to Assess Tax." (Form 872)

Internal Revenue may ask a taxpayer to sign a "consent" form if it needs more time to complete an audit. Normally, the IRS will give itself enough time to go through the entire audit process; it will not start a normal audit too close to the time barrier.

However, problems do arise. Consider a multi-year audit being conducted in March. In only a few weeks, April 15 will roll around again and the earliest return in the set being examined will become covered by the limitation rule. Unless there is fraud involved, the IRS will be unable to assess taxes on the earliest year. To cover itself, it will ask for a signature.

The taxpayer is under no obligation to sign. To do so would only expose himself to an additional assessment. However, refusing to sign the consent form could prompt the auditor to make an arbitrary tax assessment for all the deductions taken, or for an entire category of deductions. This then puts the taxpayer in the position of having to prove the validity of everything that was disallowed.

The best course of action would be to stall, to say that the matter had to be discussed with his tax advisor. And while the taxpayer and his advisor took the matter under consideration, the clock might run out on that return.

Form 872 is reproduced here, so the reader will recognize it when he sees it and not sign one by mistake.

Ten Audit Rules

Let us close this chapter with a list of 10 cardinal rules for handling an audit whenever you may be faced with one:

1. Review your return to refresh your memory. If a field audit is scheduled, or if there are many questioned items, have the return reviewed by your tax advisor.
2. Organize your records beforehand.
3. Arrange for an attorney or accountant to be present if there is a sizeable amount involved from year to year, or if imposition of criminal or civil penalties is a possibility.
4. Maintain a quiet, calm, businesslike manner throughout the proceedings.
5. Remember that candor is the best policy, but confess to nothing; misstating the facts or attempting to confuse the auditor is counterproductive.
6. Don't volunteer information; don't answer questions that are not asked; don't raise issues not in question.
7. Present only requested records; provide information only to support items under challenge.
8. Call the auditor's attention to items in your favor, such as deductions not claimed on the return; have him understand that you intend to sue for these items if the case goes to court.
9. Schedule the audit for a time and place of your own choosing.
10. Isolate the agent during a field audit by providing a stark room or office to work in, conducive only to finishing the audit as quickly as possible.

Form **872** (Rev. January 1979)	Department of the Treasury — Internal Revenue Service **Consent to Extend the Time of Assess Tax**	In Reply Refer To:

taxpayer(s) of _____
(Name(s))

_____
(Number, Street, City or Town, State, ZIP Code)

and the District Director of Internal Revenue or Regional Director of Appeals consent and agree to the following:

(1) The amount of any Federal _____ tax due on any return(s) made by
(Kind of tax)

or for the above taxpayer(s) for the period(s) ended _____

may be assessed at any time on or before _____ . However, if
(Expiration date)

a notice of deficiency in tax for any such period(s) is sent to the taxpayer(s) on or before that date, then the time for assessing the tax will be further extended by the number of days the assessment was previously prohibited, plus 60 days.

(2) This agreement ends on the earlier of the above expiration date or the assessment date of an increase in the above tax that reflects the final determination of tax and the final administrative appeals consideration. An assessment for one period covered by this agreement will not end this agreement for any other period it covers. Some assessments do not reflect a final determination and appeals consideration and therefore will not terminate the agreement before the expiration date. Examples are assessments of: (a) tax under a partial agreement; (b) tax in jeopardy; (c) tax to correct mathematical or clerical errors; (d) tax reported on amended returns; and (e) advance payments. In addition, unassessed payments, such as amounts treated by the Service as cash bonds and advance payments not assessed by the Service, will not terminate this agreement before the expiration date.

This agreement ends on the above expiration date regardless of any assessment for any period includible in a report to the Joint Committee on Taxation submitted under section 6405 of the Internal Revenue Code.

(3) The taxpayer(s) may file a claim for credit or refund and the Service may credit or refund the tax within 6 months after this agreement ends.

(SIGNATURE INSTRUCTIONS AND SPACE FOR SIGNATURE ARE ON THE BACK OF THIS FORM)

MAKING THIS CONSENT WILL NOT DEPRIVE THE TAXPAYER(S) OF ANY APPEAL RIGHTS TO WHICH THEY WOULD OTHERWISE BE ENTITLED.

YOUR SIGNATURE HERE ➔ _____   _____
                                                                                                  (Date signed)

SPOUSE'S SIGNATURE ➔ _____   _____
                                                                                                  (Date signed)

TAXPAYER'S REPRESENTATIVE
SIGN HERE ➔ _____   _____
                                                                                                  (Date signed)

CORPORATE
NAME ➔ _____

CORPORATE
OFFICER(S)   _____   _____
SIGN HERE   *(Title)*   *(Date signed)*

                _____   _____
                             (Title)   *(Date signed)*

_____   _____
DISTRICT DIRECTOR OF INTERNAL REVENUE   REGIONAL DIRECTOR OF APPEALS

BY _____   _____
                (Signature and Title)   *(Date signed)*

Instructions

If this consent is for income tax, self-employment tax, or FICA tax on tips and is made for any year(s) for which a joint return was filed, both husband and wife must sign the original and copy of this form unless one, acting under a power of attorney, signs as agent for the other. The signatures must match the names as they appear on the front of this form.

If this consent is for gift tax and the donor and the donor's spouse elected to have gifts to third persons considered as made one-half by each, both husband and wife must sign the original and copy of this form unless one, acting under a power of attorney, signs as agent for the other. The signatures must match the names as they appear on the front of this form.

If this consent is for Chapter 41, 42, or 43 taxes involving a partnership or is for a partnership return, only one authorized partner need sign.

If this consent is for Chapter 42 taxes, a separate Form 872 should be completed for each potential disqualified person, entity, or foundation manager that may be involved in a taxable transaction during the related tax year. See Revenue Ruling 75-391, 1975-2 C.B. 446.

If you are an attorney or agent of the taxpayer(s), you may sign this consent provided the action is specifically authorized by a power of attorney. If the power of attorney was not previously filed, please include it with this form.

If you are acting as a fiduciary (such as executor, administrator, trustee, etc.) and you sign this consent, attach Form 56, Notice of Fiduciary Relationship, unless it was previously filed.

If the taxpayer is a corporation, sign this consent with the corporate name followed by the signature and title of the officer(s) authorized to sign.

Form **872** (Rev 1-79)

Closing an Audit 8

Chess experts make a distinction between the game's three parts. They talk of the "opening," the "middle game," and the "end game."

In an audit, the preliminaries and the middle game (the examination itself) are likely only to cause some inconvenience and a bit of anxiety. The end game, the closing of the audit, is another matter. It is likely to be quite painful for three out of four taxpayers; this is when the auditor sums it all up and makes his assessment.

For an agent, the closing of an audit can be difficult too. There are some parallels to sales here. It is easy enough for a salesman to demonstrate his product and to explain its advantages, but much harder to get the prospect to make a decision and to get his signature on an order.

An auditor's object is the same—to get the taxpayer to acquiesce to the assessment by his signature on the consent form. He will also try to obtain immediate payment of the money due. There are likely to be objections in both cases.

When the agent feels that "all items necessary for a substantially proper determination of tax liability" have been considered, he is ready for the "close."

He will sit down with the taxpayer or his representative to spell out any proposed adjustments. The examiner is instructed to be tactful, especially when pointing out errors by the taxpayer's bookkeeper or tax preparer. When necessary, the provisions of the law supporting each adjustment will be explained.

When this review of the adjustment is completed and the bad news—the amount of the assessment—given the taxpayer, the auditor will ask the taxpayer to sign "waiver Form 870."

Form 870

Few people refer to Form 870 by its full name, "Waiver of Restrictions on Assessment and Collection of Deficiency in Tax and Acceptance of Overassessment." Though legally correct the title is probably deliberately obscure. You will hear this form called, variously, a "waiver," a "deficiency agreement," or just "Form 870."

A smart agent, and most of them are, will not make a big fuss over this form. Instead, if he senses any sort of resignation to fate or passivity on the taxpayer's part, he will probably casually say, "And I'll need your signature on this form."

You, and any other taxpayer, should not sign this form without considering its implications. First of all, a signature gives your okay to any additional assessment proposed by the auditor; if penalties or interest are charged, you agree to these too. Secondly, you consent to the immediate collection of the money due, though this does not mean you must pay on the spot.

Any taxpayer signing a waiver Form 870 shuts himself off from an important avenue of appeal, the U.S. Tax Court. Perhaps even more importantly, the opportunity for settlement on a more favorable basis along the way is closed off.

Obviously, it is to the auditor's and Internal Revenue's advantage to obtain a taxpayer's "John Hancock." The agent gets credit for closing out the audit without a "no change," the IRS saves the costs of appeal and can speed up its collection process, and it can add another taxpayer to a favorable statistical column.

It may or may not be to the taxpayer's advantage to sign the 870. There is even a small possibility that the examiner may have discovered an "over-assessment"; the taxpayer may have paid too much. If you have previously decided to file an amended return to claim the over-assessment now conceded by the agent, it might be a good idea to sign. This will make unnecessary another rehash of the matter already favorably decided in your favor by the agent when the refund claim is later processed by a different individual.

If the audit ends with the agent proposing additional taxes as part of the settlement and if the amount is not too large, it also might be simpler and cheaper to sign on the bottom line. So too, if the assessment is within the limits of what you and your advisor have determined to be realistic after your pre-audit review of the tax return. The "adverse" audit result may actually be more favorable than the taxpayer had reason to believe was possible. Another troublesome issue may have been missed completely. An 870 may become the stamp of approval on a serious tax problem extending over several years. However, an adverse result should not be accepted even if the taxpayer thinks it is not too bad, without

talking to a tax expert about any big ticket item resolved in the IRS' favor. The IRS may have been dead wrong on this item, or have missed the point because of poor explanation by the taxpayer.

In any case, waiver Form 870 is a one-way deal. If you sign, you agree to the assessment, but the IRS does not bind itself in any way at this particular stage of the proceedings. All audit results are reviewed; a tax auditor's or revenue agent's proposed assessment is not final until after this review. His supervisor may revise the findings. IRS Manual 4231 states, ". . . the agent will adopt the supervisor's position as his/her own. Under no circumstances will the agent let the taxpayer or his/her representative know that he/she may have reservations about the new position."

If, however, upon review, the IRS approves the deal, it cannot reopen the matter with another audit of the same year's return. And, if the same issue is questioned on audit the next year, the taxpayer has a strong argument for resolving it in the same way.

If you do sign, the agent will ask you to pay the amount of the assessment on the spot. He presumes you have your checkbook with you. Again, you have options; you may pay now or you may wait for a bill from Internal Revenue. If you do pay, interest is charged from the day the return was due (generally April 15 of the year the return was filed) to the date you actually pay. The agent will certainly point out to you that you will save on interest charges by paying sooner than later.

If you do not sign, the agent will advise you of your appeal rights, both inside the IRS and outside, in the courts. He will then gather your case jacket and his worksheets, for this is the end of his (but not the IRS') direct involvement with you. You should take this opportunity to use this pause in the proceedings to consult an expert on the big items resolved for and against you, to determine whether the Form 870 should, in fact, be signed.

Thirty-day Letter

At a later date, you will receive by mail a copy of the agent's audit report explaining his proposed adjustments, and a letter advising you of your right to appeal within 30 days. Publication 5, "Appeal Rights and Preparation of Protests for Unagreed Cases," will also be enclosed. Ever hopeful of resolving the matter as quickly and inexpensively as possible, the IRS will also include another copy of Form 870. It may be that after talking with your tax advisor, you will decide that now is the time to sign the waiver form, to avoid other problems surfacing as your case wends its way up the appeal ladder.

(The matter of appeals is discussed in Chapters 11 and 12, and you will learn then that in the great majority of cases, the chances of settlement improve as a case moves up the ladder, particularly where several issues are involved or the facts are complicated.)

Ninety-day Letter

If a taxpayer does not pay or make an appeal within the 30-day period, he will receive yet another letter. This is officially called the "Statutory Notice of Deficiency," and comes with several pages of back-up documentation. Commonly called the "90-day letter," it tells the taxpayer that he must either take his case to Tax Court or pay up within 90 days of the date the letter was mailed.

The importance of the 90-day letter is that it sets a final time limit for action; its other significant content, the amount of the proposed deficiency, was probably already transmitted, together with the Revenue Agent's Report (RAR), by the preceeding 30-day letter. (If you successfully challenged an item on the 30-day letter, of course, the amounts will differ to the extent of the favorable adjustment.)

You can challenge a 90-day letter's validity, or even deliberately choose to disregard it, but it should not be ignored. In the context of a tax audit and its resultant financial problems, the 90-day letter is a critical communication. You have less than 90 days to get your act together, either to consult with tax professionals and to prepare a Tax Court petition, or to pay the taxes due together with any interest and penalties involved.

The reason is that the 90-day letter is "jurisdictional"; it is specifically mentioned in the Internal Revenue Code. The Tax Court does not have jurisdiction if you do not file your petition within the prescribed 90-day period, even though the statute of limitations may have months or years yet to run. The Tax Court, Internal Revenue itself, not even the Supreme Court, can help you if you fail to petition the Tax Court in time.

Here is the actual text of a 90-day letter: "This letter is a NOTICE OF DEFICIENCY. We have determined the income tax deficiencies shown above. We are sorry that we could not reach a satisfactory agreement with you. The enclosed statement shows how we computed the deficiencies.

If you decide not to contest our determination in the United States Tax Court, we would appreciate it if you would sign and return the enclosed Statutory Notice Statement. This will permit us to assess the deficiencies quickly and will limit the accumulation of interest. The enclosed self-addressed envelope is for your convenience.

If you decide not to sign and return the statement, the law requires us to assess and bill you for the deficiencies after 90 days from the date of mailing this letter (150 days if the letter is addressed to you outside the United States). However, if you contest this determination by filing a petition within that time with the United States Tax Court, 400 Second

Street, NW, Washington, DC 20217, we may not assess any deficiencies and bill you until after the Tax Court has decided your case. You can obtain a copy of the rules for filing a petition by writing to the Clerk of the Tax Court at the Court's Washington, DC address stated above. *The time within which you may file a petition with the Court (90 or 150 days, as the case may be) is fixed by law, and the Court cannot consider your case if the petition is filed late.*

If you have any questions, please contact the person whose name and telephone number are shown above."

Stopping the Interest Clock

All the while that Internal Revenue is sending letters and the taxpayer pondering which course to follow, the interest clock is continuing to run.

There is another option besides paying or appealing during the 90-day statutory period. The taxpayer can pay the tax assessed and the interest due up to the payment date. Then he can file an amended return to claim a refund on all or part of the money paid. Since he has paid the tax, any further interest accumulation stops immediately.

In post-audit situations, a taxpayer has two years from the date of this tax payment to file an amended return. Form 1040X is suitable for a taxpayer seeking a refund of taxes due to payment of a tax deficiency.

An amended return, of course, will be examined again by Internal Revenue. It technically opens up the whole process again. Even a compromise agreement with the IRS becomes possible.

Form **870** (Rev. 3-78)	Department of the Treasury · Internal Revenue Service **Waiver of Restrictions on Assessment and Collection of Deficiency in Tax and Acceptance of Overassessment**	Date received by Internal Revenue Service

I consent to the immediate assessment and collection of any deficiencies (increase in tax and penalties) and accept any overassessment (decrease in tax and penalties) shown below, plus any interest provided by law. I understand that by signing this waiver, I will not be able to contest these years in the United States Tax Court, unless additional deficiencies are determined for these years.

Increase in Tax and Penalties

Taxable year ended	Amount of tax	Penalty

Decrease in Tax and Penalties

Taxable year ended	Amount of tax	Penalty

Names and address of taxpayers *(Number, street, city or town, State, ZIP code)*

Signature	Title *(If applicable)*	Date
Signature	Title *(If applicable)*	Date
Signature By	Title	Date

NOTE: If you consent to the assessment of the deficiencies shown in this waiver, please sign and return the form in order to limit any interest charge and expedite the adjustment to your account. Your consent will not prevent you from filing a claim for refund (after you have paid the tax) if you later believe you are so entitled; nor prevent us from later determining, if necessary, that you owe additional tax; nor extend the time provided by law for either action.

If you later file a claim and the Service disallows it, you may file suit for refund in a district court or in the United States Court of Claims, but you may not file a petition with the United States Tax Court.

We will consider this waiver a valid claim for refund or credit of any overpayment due you resulting from any decrease in tax and penalties determined by the Internal Revenue Service, shown above, provided you sign and file it within the period established by law for making such a claim.

Who Must Sign: If you filed jointly, both you and your spouse must sign. If this waiver is for a corporation, it should be signed with the corporation name, followed by the signatures and titles of the corporate officers authorized to sign. An attorney or agent may sign this waiver provided such action is specifically authorized by a power of attorney which, if not previously filed, must accompany this form.

If this waiver is signed by a person acting in a fiduciary capacity (for example, an executor, administrator, or a trustee) Form 56, Notice of Fiduciary Relationship, should, unless previously filed, accompany this form.

Form **870** (Rev. 3-78)

Criminal Audits 9

Civil audits and criminal audits are two different games. They may appear alike to the uninitiated, but they are played to entirely different rules. An analogy might be the difference between checkers and chess.

In a run-of-the-mill civil audit conducted by examination division personnel, the burden of proof is on the taxpayer. He must prove to Internal Revenue that his self-assessed tax is correct as filed. If the case goes on to court, the taxpayer still bears the burden of proving, by the "preponderance of evidence," every factual element of his case. That is, unless the IRS has alleged "civil tax fraud," in which case the burden on this issue alone is on the IRS.

In a criminal audit, and later in court, the IRS has the task of proving that the taxpayer committed a tax crime. Proof of every element of the alleged crime must be proven "beyond a reasonable doubt." In criminal tax cases, the IRS is represented in court by the Justice Department, which acts as the IRS' law firm.

Auditors are, in a sense, tax adjustors; their work resembles that of insurance adjustors. They basically challenge taxpayers' claims and try to pick up a few extra dollars in taxes.

In contrast, special agents from the Criminal Investigation Division are tax policemen; their work parallels that of detectives on a large police force. Special agents investigate tax crimes and collect evidence to be used in court against suspected taxpayers. According to the IRS "Handbook for Special Agents," an agent's "primary aim is to determine whether the person under investigation has committed a criminal violation and, if the facts disclose violations subject to criminal or civil penalties within the jurisdiction of the Intelligence Division, to obtain whatever evidence is required to sustain criminal proceedings or the assertion of civil penalties."

Special agents write reports which form the paperwork foundation of federal prosecutors' cases. Most criminal tax cases are presented to a grand jury, but in some cases, special agents file "complaints," sworn written statements, directly with United States magistrates. In response to such a complaint, a magistrate may issue a summons compelling a taxpayer to appear before him to answer the charges. Or a warrant may be issued instead, in which case a special agent arrests the taxpayer and physically brings him before the magistrate.

When this procedure is used, the initial appearance before a magistrate is short and a formality. A date is set for a preliminary examination "to determine whether there is probable cause to believe that an offense has been committed and that the arrested person committed it." Depending upon the circumstances, the suspect may be held in custody, or a bail bond required for his release until the

Exhibit 600-1

Complaint
Handbook Reference: Subsection 625.1

◇

IN THE DISTRICT COURT OF THE UNITED STATES
FOR THE _____ DISTRICT OF _____

UNITED STATES OF AMERICA   )
)
        —against—   )   COMPLAINT
)
_____   )

Complaint for Violation of Section 7201,
Internal Revenue Code of 1954

Before _____, United States Magistrate. _____,
_____.

The undersigned complainant, being duly sworn, states:

That he/she is a Special Agent (or Revenue Agent) of the Internal Revenue Service and, in the performance of the duties imposed on him/her by law, he/she has conducted an investigation of the Federal income tax liability of _____ _____ for the calendar year 19____, by examining the said taxpayer's tax return for the year 19____ and other years; (by examination and audit of the said taxpayer's business and financial books and records;) (by identifying and interviewing third parties with whom the said taxpayer did business;) (by consulting public and private records reflecting the said taxpayer's income,) (and by interviewing third persons having knowledge of the said taxpayer's financial condition).

That based on the aforesaid investigation, the complainant has personal knowledge that on or about the _____ day of _____, 19____, at _____, _____, in the _____ District of _____, _____ (who during the calendar year 19____ was married) did willfully and knowingly attempt to evade and defeat a large part of the income tax due and owing by said taxpayer (and spouse) to the United States of America for the calendar year 19____, by filing and causing to be filed with the Director of Internal Revenue at _____, _____, a false and fraudulent (joint) income tax return (on behalf of said taxpayer and spouse), wherein he/she (it was) stated that his/her (their) taxable (or adjusted gross) income for the said calendar year 19____ was $_____, and that the amount of tax due and owing thereon was the sum of $_____, when in fact his/her (their joint) taxable (or adjusted gross) income for the said calendar year was the sum of $_____, upon which said taxable income he/she owed (there was owing) to the United States of America an income tax of $_____.

_____
Here type: Title of subscribing Internal
Revenue Service Officer

Sworn to before me and subscribed in my presence, this _____ day of _____, 19____.

_____
United States Magistrate

The bracketed descriptions of the kinds of investigations conducted by the subscribing agent may all be used if they correctly reflect the facts. Otherwise, the inapposite description should, of course, be deleted. When appropriate, the description of a different investigative course should be added or substituted based on the facts.

This form in adaptable for use in connection with situations where either an individual or a joint tax return has been filed. The bracketed portions in the second paragraph relate to a joint tax return and should be deleted if an individual return is involved.

examination.

If the taxpayer (or non-taxpayer) is kept in custody, the hearing must be held within 10 days. If released, the examination must take place no later than 20 days after the initial appearance before the magistrate.

This preliminary hearing is not a trial, but the IRS may produce witnesses, the accused may cross-examine them and introduce evidence in his own favor. It is up to the magistrate to decide if there is probable cause to believe the accused has committed an offense, to discharge him, or to send the case along to federal district court. The accused may waive the preliminary hearing, in which case the case goes directly to court.

Because a defendant does not have a right to appear as a witness, Internal Revenue prefers to begin most tax cases before a federal grand jury. If an indictment is returned against a taxpayer, no hearing is necessary. Alternatively, an "information," a sworn accusation in writing, may be filed in federal court by a U.S. attorney, which also makes a hearing legally unnecessary.

A special agent who recommends prosecution and whose recommendation is upheld, ends up assisting a U.S. attorney in the presentation of a case before a grand jury. He reviews and prepares the case with the attorney, and assists in the preparation of the indictment form, and testifies before the grand jurors. Legally, a grand jury may return an indictment based solely upon a special agent's testimony and, the grand jury system being what it is, will almost always indict.

An agent's role continues right into the courtroom of a U.S. district court. A special agent may be asked to help prepare a "trial brief" or "trial book," that organizes the miscellaneous statements, affidavits, memoranda of interviews, and witness sheets that document the government's case. A special agent may check with witnesses before a trial begins, to insure that documents or other

evidence is all at hand, or that they recall their previous statements. He is expected to inform the prosecuting attorney of any difficulties that might arise with witnesses, such as hostility that may be prejudicial to the government's case. The special agent, himself, will testify as a witness before the court.

According to the special agent's handbook, while the trial is in progress, "The Special Agent should listen carefully to all testimony, making notes from which he/she may alert the United States Attorney... as to any false, misleading, or erroneous statements. The agent may also assist in preparing questions to be asked defense witnesses on cross-examination."

In short, it is the special agent's job to see that a court convicts whomever the special agent recommends be prosecuted.

What is a Tax Crime?

Tax crimes generally involve tax evasion as distinct from tax avoidance.

Tax avoidance, the manipulation, within legal limits, of a taxpayer's financial affairs so as to minimize tax liability, is allowable. Tax evasion is breaking the law one way or another. It is often said that the difference between tax avoidance and tax evasion is $10,000 plus five years.

But the matter is not a joking one to taxpayers accused of evasion. The real question is whether the taxpayer intended to break the law, was "willful" in his attempt.

The IRS itself makes the distinction in the Special Agents' Handbook as follows:

Avoidance Distinguished from Evasion
"Avoidance of taxes is not a criminal offense. Any attempt to reduce, avoid, minimize, or alleviate taxes by legitimate means is permissible. The distinction between evasion and avoidance is fine yet definite. One who avoids tax does not conceal or misrepresent. He shapes events to reduce or

Exhibit 600-2

Indictment
Handbook Reference: Subsection 625.1

◇

INDICTMENT

IN THE DISTRICT COURT OF THE UNITED STATES

FOR THE _____ DISTRICT OF _____

UNITED STATES OF AMERICA   )
—against—   )
_____)

No. _____

    (26 United States Code
    Section 7201)

The grand jury charges:

That on or about the _____ day of _____, 19____, in the _____ District of _____, _____, late of _____, did willfully and knowingly attempt to evade and defeat a large part of the income tax due and owing by him/her in the United States of America for the calendar year 19____, by filing and causing to be filed with the Director of Internal Revenue for the _____, Internal Revenue District of _____, at _____, a false and fraudulent income tax return wherein he/she stated that his/her taxable income for said calendar year was the sum of $_____ and that the amount of tax due and owing thereon was the sum of $_____, whereas, as he/she then and there well knew, his/her taxable income for the said calendar year was the sum of $_____, upon which said net income he/she owed to the United States of America an income tax of $_____.

In violation of Section 7201, Internal Revenue Code; 26 U.S.C., Section 7201.

                A True Bill.

            _____

                Foreman

_____

United States Attorney

Exhibit 600-3

Information
Handbook Reference: Subsection 621   ◇

INFORMATION

IN THE DISTRICT COURT OF THE UNITED STATES
FOR THE _____ DISTRICT OF _____

UNITED STATES OF AMERICA   )   No. _____
—against—   )
_____   )   (26 United States Code
                                           Section 7203)

The United States Attorney charges:

That during the calendar year 19___, _____, who was a resident of the City of _____, State of _____, had and received a gross income of $_____; that by reason of such income he/she was required by law, after the close of the calendar year 19___, and on or before April 15, 19___, to make an income tax return to the Director of Internal Revenue for the _____ Internal Revenue District of _____, stating specifically the items of his/her gross income and any deductions and credits to which he/she was entitled; that well knowing all of the foregoing facts, he/she did willfully and knowingly fail to make said income tax return to the said Director of Internal Revenue, or to any other proper officer of the United States.

In violation of Section 7203, Internal Revenue Code; 26 U.S.C. Section 7203

_____
United States Attorney

eliminate tax liability and upon the happening of the events, makes a complete disclosure. Evasion, on the other hand, involves deceit, subterfuge, camouflage, concealment, some attempt to color or obscure events, or making things seem other than what they are."

Perhaps the best way to clarify what the government considers tax crimes is to itemize the most common criminal provisions of the Internal Revenue Code. (There are others, but these are the ones involved in the great majority of income tax cases.)

Attempt to Evade or Defeat Tax (IRC 7201): "Any person who willfully attempts in any manner to evade or defeat any tax imposed by this title or the payment thereof shall . . . be guilty of a felony and upon conviction thereof, shall be fined not more than $10,000, or imprisoned not more than 5 years, or both, together with the costs of prosecution."

Willful Failure to Collect or Pay Over Tax (IRC 7202): "Any person required under this title to collect, account for, and pay over any tax imposed by this title who willfully fails to collect or truthfully account for and pay over such tax shall . . . be guilty of a felony." This usually has application to cases involving withholding taxes of employees. Penalties are the same as for IRC 7201.

Willful Failure to File Return, Supply Information, or Pay Tax (IRC 7203): "Any person required under this title to pay any estimated tax or tax required . . . to make a return . . . keep any records, or supply any information, who willfully fails (to do so,) shall . . . be guilty of a misdemeanor and, upon conviction thereof, shall be fined not more than $10,000 or imprisoned not more than one year, or both."

Fraudulent Withholding Exemption Certificate or Failure to Supply Information (IRC 7205): Any individual required to supply information to his employer . . . who willfully supplies false or fraudulent information, or who willfully fails to supply information . . . which would require an increase in the tax to be withheld, shall . . . be fined not more than $500 or imprisoned not more than one year, or both."

Fraud and False Statements (IRC 7206): This is a broad provision. A declaration or statement not believed "to be true and correct as to every material matter, (made) under the penalties of perjury," is a violation. This normally would include every formal interview or statement made to a special agent or an auditor. Giving aid or assistance in the preparation of a fraudulent return, affidavit, claim, or document is also against this law.

Withholding, falsifying or destroying records, or concealing property in connection with a compromise or closing agreement also comes under this provision. Conviction of violating any of these strictures is punishable by up to $5,000 and three years.

This section is perhaps more important than any other, since a special agent can use it to create a case where none would have otherwise existed; all that he needs is for a taxpayer to lie to him because the true answer to one of his questions would have been embarrassing.

Fraudulent Returns, Statements, or Other Documents (IRC 7202): "Any person who willfully delivers or discloses . . . any list, return, account, statement, or other document, known by him to be fraudulent or to be false as to any material matter, shall be fined not more than $1,000, or imprisoned not more than one year, or both."

This is the backup misdemeanor charge to Section 7201, in case a district court refuses to convict the taxpayer of a felony. It is also used extensively in plea bargaining.

Failure to Obey Summons (IRC 7210): Failure to appear or to produce records when summoned by an IRS agent calls for the same penalties as 7207. You can contest a summons, but do not ignore one.

The U.S. Code

The Internal Revenue Service is only part of the government and its agents only one category of federal agent. In dealing with the Internal Revenue, it is possible to run afoul of provisions of the more general U.S. Code. Violations of the U.S. Code will also be pursued by the IRS if discovered as part of a tax investigation.

Penalties are sometimes higher under the U.S. Code than for breaking provisions of the tax law.

Assaulting, Resisting, or Impeding Certain Officers or Employees (USC 111): A conviction under this provision can bring down a penalty of up to $10,000, and 10 years imprisonment if a deadly or dangerous weapon is involved. If not, a fine of up to $5,000 or three years imprisonment, or both, is the rule.

Offer to Officer or Other Person (USC 201): A bribe or the offer of one will get a taxpayer a fine of three times the money involved, or up to three years, or both.

False, Fictitious, or Fraudulent Claims (USC 287): This provision can be used as a backup to the tax laws—$10,000, five years.

Conspiracy to Commit Offense or to Defraud the United States (USC 371): It is not necessary to actually commit a violation, only for two or more persons to plan and to take any steps towards committing an offense, to come under this provision. Penalties can be up to $10,000 and five years.

Statements or Entries Generally (USC 1001): This is another catch-all provision, appropriately numbered. "Whoever . . . knowingly and willfully falsifies, conceals or covers up by any trick, scheme, or device a material fact . . . shall be fined not more than $10,000 or

imprisoned not more than five years, or both."

Racketeer Influenced and Corrupt Organizations (USC 1962, 1963): "A pattern of racketeering activity or collection of unlawful debt" will permit prosecution under this law. Penalties are heavy—up to $25,000 in fines, to 20 years imprisonment, and forfeiture of any property or other interests acquired in violation of Section 1962.

The Threat

There are many more provisions of the Internal Revenue Code and the U.S. Code that can be used to pin down suspected tax violators. The ones listed here are only given as examples of the threat. But do not permit an auditor or a special agent to use the threat of criminal prosecution for a multiplicity of tax crimes to cajole you into agreeing to additional tax assessments. Remember that "one who avoids does not conceal or misrepresent." If you have disclosed the facts on your tax return, generally speaking, you have nothing to worry about in terms of fraud or other criminal offenses. Don't let an empty threat hassle you, but do call in an attorney. This is usually the only way to call this sort of bluff by an over-zealous agent.

In a tax case, the IRS and the federal prosecuting attorney (usually an assistant U.S. attorney, but sometimes the U.S. attorney for the district, or even a specialist from the Tax Division of the Justice Department) will normally charge an offender with the violation of as many provisions as possible.

This is not a bluff, nor is it necessarily a real threat. As the case progresses through the U.S. District Court (where all tax crimes are tried), some of the charges will almost certainly be dropped by the court or by the government's attorneys. Perhaps the prosecution will bargain, accepting a guilty plea to one or more lesser charges in exchange for not pursuing others. A plea of "no contest" may be accepted by some U.S. attorneys, but not by others. It may be possible to submit a "stipulation of facts" to the court, which makes conviction for a lesser offense (a misdemeanor) a certainty, but eliminates the entry of a guilty plea, or conviction, for more serious offenses.

To sum up, the idea with which a special agent enters an investigation is to get a relatively certain conviction on some charge, no matter which one.

The greatest dangers in terms of the threat of criminal prosecution for tax crimes are that blind fear of prosecution for nonprovable offenses will lead to false statements under oath, (all statements to an IRS agent are, in effect, under oath), and that panic about discovery of omitted income or overstated expenses, which may not even be willful and, hence, criminal, will lead to document destruction, persuading witnesses to commit perjury, or even bribery. In each instance, the crime becomes a more serious one and easier to prove. If you have any doubts about what to do when threatened with tax prosecution, first reread IRC sections 7206 and 7207 and USC sections 1001 and 201, and then call your attorney. Above all, if questioned, advise all your friends, family and acquaintances to tell the truth.

Actual Prosecution

To be successfully prosecuted for tax fraud or another tax law violation is to be a member of a select and unlucky minority.

In 1978, only 9,481 cases were initiated by the Criminal Investigation Division. Investigations were completed in 8,713 cases and prosecution of 3,439 taxpayers recommended.

Many of these were dropped by the IRS Chief Counsel's office, declined by the Justice Department, or acquitted by a grand jury. Prosecution was "successfully" completed (for the IRS) in only 1,414 cases. Of these, 1,056 taxpayers pleaded guilty; 133 "no

contest" or *nolo contendere* (which means not admitting guilt but not making a defense either). Only 224 were convicted after a trial. Of those sentenced during 1978, 47.1 percent (or 681 in all) were sentenced to prison terms.

The small proportion of taxpayers investigated that are recommended for prosecution, and the relatively high number pleading guilty are worthy of note. Most of the IRS is generally more interested in money than in convictions. Many of these cases were settled and dropped, the threat of court convincing some taxpayers that the time to argue was over. It is also difficult to prove the element of "willfulness" in fraud cases; the great majority of dropped charges in the criminal tax area are not prosecuted because of doubts that a conviction "beyond a reasonable doubt" can likely be obtained. In fact, once an investigation is begun, a low likelihood of a conviction is the only significant reason the great majority of cases are not taken to court.

This does not mean that those investigated but not convicted and sentenced got off free. For every criminal fraud investigation there is usually a parallel civil audit, which will almost always lag behind the criminal case.

When a criminal case is dropped as unworthy of prosecution because it will be difficult to prove a violation to the satisfaction of a court, making conviction unlikely, the civil case remains open. If the IRS does not always win its criminal prosecutions, it usually tries to make up on the civil side.

However, if Internal Revenue wins on the criminal side, it still goes ahead with the civil case. It will try for a conviction on civil fraud, which demands a lower level of proof ("clear and convincing" evidence is enough), and will assess negligence penalties where applicable.

The important point is that the two sides of a serious tax case, criminal and civil, are independent in function but cumulative in application. While special agents investigate and lawyers make up their minds, interest and civil penalties continue to pile up. And eventually, the Collection Division takes its toll. Many a taxpayer has won his criminal case, perhaps even being found not guilty of fraud, only to find himself still facing a civil fraud case and owing money to Internal Revenue for penalties and interest.

Special Enforcement Program

Internal Revenue's criminal investigation activity is divided into two programs: a "General Program" and a "Special Enforcement Program."

As might be expected, the General Program deals with the common taxpayer gone astray. Within this program are special projects concentrating on such areas as questionable refunds and "illegal" tax protesters.

The Special Enforcement Program concentrates on identifying and investigating persons "who derive substantial income from illegal activities." The tax laws are used as a weapon in the federal government's war against criminal profiteers, organized or not.

Because there is a booming and profitable traffic in narcotics of all kinds, there is a special project within the special program dedicated to the drug trade. Leads are provided by other agencies, such as the Drug Enforcement Administration. If the DEA can't catch smugglers with the goods, the IRS tries to catch them with the money. During 1978, 378 drug-related criminal tax investigations were completed and 65 indictments and 56 convictions obtained.

IRS special agents are also assigned to the Federal Organized Crime and Strike Force Program. Units of the strike force combine agents and investigators from several federal agencies in an anti-organized-crime effort. Since 1966, this program has successfully prosecuted 941 people for tax violations.

Internal Revenue's history as a government anti-crime weapon goes back much further, though. On October 24, 1931, Chicago's infamous free enterpriser Al Capone was sentenced to 11 years in a federal penitentiary—for tax evasion. This was the only charge the government could successfully use to prosecute Capone.

Discovery of Fraud

Most cases of tax fraud are first discovered by ordinary tax auditors or revenue agents during routine audits.

Since fraud is largely concealment and misrepresentation, uncovering it depends mostly upon the auditor's thoroughness. If the records presented by the taxpayer and his explanations in response to an examiner's queries are accepted with only casual verification, any hanky-panky is likely to remain undiscovered.

Experienced agents often claim that their "intuition" is important in recognizing fraud. More likely, they subconsciously respond to the hints, the incongruities, that a less seasoned auditor would have to deliberately seek out.

The first hints of the possibility of tax fraud can be found in the sources of income of a taxpayer or business. Some occupations have the potential for high income; reported income inconsistent with normal expectations might alert an auditor. The possibility of "windfall" profits because of unusual business conditions might be a signal. Businesses that deal largely in cash are always suspect. Anyone in an influential positon, with the potential for bribes or graft, may be tempted. Strong vibrations are given off by small business where the owners control both the income and the records.

Leads may also turn up in a taxpayer's file. Prior audit reports, fraud investigations in past years and notes of the unconfirmed suspicions of other examiners will perk up the ears of the densest auditor. A file might also include reports from other federal agencies, state tax bureaus, information from banks on large currency transactions, and even accusations from an informant.

A conscientious auditor conducting his pre-examination research might arm himself with ratios (investment to income, expenses against sales, and the like) normal for a particular taxpayer's industry. These ratios compared with the tax return under question could also arouse suspicions.

Elsewhere in this book, the advantages of handling an audit through a tax advisor on his professional premises, if possible, have been discussed. Where income has been understated by whatever means, such a procedure could be of critical importance.

On an initial contact, the first interview with a taxpayer, auditors are expected to review his financial situation and to be alert for an indication of potential fraud. A taxpayer's home and its furnishings are evaluated for signs of unreported prosperity. A business is eyeballed to judge traffic compared with reported sales. A professional's office is inspected and note made of activity, staff, furnishings, equipment and clientele.

Personal conversation with a taxpayer can provide leads for investigation. Internal Revenue's "Audit Technique Handbook" specifically instructs agents, "During this discussion taxpayers frequently disclose much information concerning themselves and their finances which will be useful to the agent in making the audit. The taxpayers may also inadvertently reveal information leading to unreported income."

A taxpayer's behavior during the audit proper can provide clues to a receptive agent. Procrastination, stalling, and an uncooperative attitude when records or explanations are requested are patterns that might tell an auditor to dig deeper. Poor or inadequate books spell trouble too. Altered records or faked documentation are signals of possible fraud. Not using bank acounts, disbursements in cash, not regularly depositing all income, can also be symptomatic of problems. The legitimate taxpayer who doesn't like using banks or writing checks, or who just likes to deal in cash, is the bane of tax attorneys because guilt can be imputed where none exists. An infallible sign, obvious to most experienced auditors, is the unwillingness of a taxpayer who runs a fair-sized enterprise to delegate control of receipts to an employee. Ironically, anxiety, a willingness to agree to any deficiency to get the agent off the premises, flag a taxpayer for a more concentrated effort.

None of these, in themselves, constitutes evidence of tax fraud. They may, instead, be just evidence of poor business practice or personality problems. But they are things that arouse an agent's suspicions, especially when two or more signals are flashed by the same taxpayer. The taxpayer who regularly deals in cash not only flashes several signals at once; he also presents an inviting target for both a civil and a criminal audit; because proof of his deductions is likely to be unavailable.

Referral to Intelligence

Suspicion of fraud is not enough to justify referral of a case to the Criminal Investigation Division. An auditor must first find firm indications of fraud, and then develop them enough to be able to provide sufficient information to the Investigation Division.

The auditor is supposed to gather whatever information he needs to support his suspicions without alerting the taxpayer. Undue emphasis is not to be placed on obtaining records related to the suspicious items; an agent may mask his intentions by requesting unrelated material at the same time. When questioning a taxpayer about such an item, the auditor should not press or make a detailed interrogation, but only go so far as necessary to support an indication of fraud.

To the IRS, there are two prime indications of fraud: first, that there has been a substantial understatement of taxable income or over- statement of expenses or deductions; and second, that the taxpayer cannot explain the apparent discrepancies, or that the explana- tion offered is not plausible.

Auditors are instructed to suspend the audit "at the earliest point, after discovering firm indications of fraud." They are to do this without alarming the taxpayer or disclosing the reason for the suspension to the taxpayer.

A Form 2797, "Referral Report for Poten- tial Fraud Cases," is then prepared. This summarizes the auditor's reasons for believing a tax fraud case may exist. The Criminal Investigation Division uses this referral report as the basis for its decision whether to mount a fuller investigation or not.

Until Investigation decides to accept or decline the referral, the audit will remain suspended, and the auditor will not have any contact with the suspect taxpayer.

Joint Investigation

If the Criminal Investigation Division accepts the referral, the auditor will, in all probability, return. This time he will be accompanied by a special agent and a "joint investigation" for tax fraud will have begun. The tip-off will be a time lag, followed by the appearance of an unfamiliar face. At this moment, a taxpayer's entire posture towards the IRS must change; he no longer is obligated by law or custom to be cooperative.

A joint investigation is a team effort by the Examination and Investigation divisions to determine the taxpayer's correct tax liability, any liability for civil penalties, and whether criminal prosecution should be sought. Natu- rally, the responsibilities of the two agents overlap somewhat. Neither agent is in charge, though the interests of Investigation normally

take priority.

The IRS "Audit Technique Handbook" is enlightening on this point: "Because of the importance of a criminal case from the deter- rent standpoint in buttressing voluntary com- pliance, the criminal aspect predominates in a joint investigation."

Management authority for the investigation rests jointly with the group managers of the two agents. Normally, the revenue agent will be responsible for the examination and verifi- cation of accounts. This is an intensive exten- sion of regular audit routine. If the taxpayer's records are inadequate, the revenue officer will make the computations necessary to estimate the taxpayer's true income, and the taxes and civil penalties due.

The special agent has the responsibility for the criminal aspects of the investigation. He will develop the evidence necessary to prove a criminal violation. His duties include inter- rogating witnesses, obtaining admissions from the suspect taxpayer, and properly document- ing records and transactions essential to the case.

Separate Investigation

If the Investigation Division does not accept the referral, the auditor will return alone to pick up the examination where he left off.

Such "separate investigations" can also arise when a special agent withdraws from a joint investigation because he determines that there is no criminal potential to be developed. Sometimes, too, the Investigation Division will refer a fresh case to the Examination Division after it evaluates a return as having audit potential but no criminal fraud elements.

If, in the course of his continued audit, the revenue officer uncovers new and stronger evidence of tax fraud, the case may be referred again to Investigation. This is unlikely, but possible.

Signals to a Taxpayer

The strongest signal possible to a taxpayer that he is about to undergo a criminal audit is the appearance of a special agent at his door. The procedure to follow was outlined before: always ask for identification and call a tax attorney immediately.

But there also are weaker signals that might possibly be picked up by an alert taxpayer. When an auditor suspects fraud but has not yet firmed up his indications and broken off contact, he may increase the pace of his note-taking. An auditor's instructions for such situations include making "contemporaneous notes of all contacts with the taxpayer, his/her employees, or third parties, showing date, time of day, place, and exact words, if possible." Normally, any note-taking will relate more directly to the papers and numbers before him.

As advised before, a log of records requested by and provided to an auditor is a good idea. If an examiner breaks off contact unexpectedly without a plausible reason, review the log sheets. A concentration of requests for supporting paperwork in an area known to be sensitive might well be a signal that the case is being referred. A consultation with your attorney might well be timely if this occurs.

Proving Violations

Whenever a taxpayer is charged with a criminal violation of a tax law, the government has a problem. It must prove every facet of the charged offense and demonstrate the taxpayer's guilt to the court beyond a reasonable doubt.

As an example, let us consider IRC 7201, "willfully attempting in any manner to evade or defeat any tax. . . ." The government has the task of proving three elements of this offense: that there are additional taxes due and owing; that an attempt was made to evade and defeat any tax; and willfulness.

For the first element, the government must establish that "the taxpayer owed more tax than he reported." There are several accepted methods of doing this, even in the absence of adequate records. (See the next section on "Methods of Proof.")

An "attempt in any manner" is the key to the second element. Prior court decisions have held that attempts cover both successful and unsuccessful, or futile, endeavors or efforts. The courts have ruled "that the term 'attempt' implies some affirmative action or the commission of some overt act."

"Willfulness," the third element, is more difficult to prove and probably the element that causes the IRS to decide not to prosecute many potential criminal cases. Understatement of income or an incorrect return does "not in itself constitute willful attempted tax evasion." According to one court decision, willfulness is "an act of conduct done with bad or evil purpose."

If a criminal violation, with a possible penalty of imprisonment, cannot be proven, the civil case is likely to remain open and still provable. Acquittal or dismissal of a criminal tax case does not decide a parallel civil tax action. But conviction on a criminal tax violation will probably prove fraud in the civil case.

Methods of Proof

To prove that a taxpayer understated his income, it is necessary to establish what correct taxable income should have been reported. This is not always a simple task, especially in the absence of adequate records.

The most common method used by special agents to prove a taxpayer's real income is the "specific item method." It has the advantages of being easily presented in court and of being comprehensible to jurors lacking an accounting education.

Under this method, the IRS demonstrates

that a taxpayer took fictitious deductions, claimed false exemptions or tax credits, or omitted income when filing his return. "Omitted income" can be salaries, gains from the sale of property, commissions, fees, or dividends. Sales revenue not reported is the most common violation of this sort by businesses.

The "net worth method" is the second most common way Internal Revenue establishes that a taxpayer has had unreported income. Basically, this involves proving that a taxpayer's net worth has grown faster than would have been possible if his income were as reported on his tax returns.

To do this, the investigators must fix a taxpayer's net worth at a "starting point," a date prior to the tax period under question. A financial statement presented to a bank as part of a credit application might simplify the agents' task. Otherwise, they will resort to bank and brokerage house records, real estate records, prior tax returns, credit reports, and the taxpayer's own account books or papers from past years.

The most common taxpayer parry to the net worth method is to claim that he possessed a "cash hoard" from which his later prosperity was financed. To negate this defense, the IRS will also try to document that such funds did not exist. They will use such evidence as bounced checks, bankruptcy proceedings, a history of installment buying or slow payment of debts, and a defendant's history of low earnings to make their point.

A net worth statement compiled from the same sort of sources as the first computation will be made for a date at the end of the tax years under scrutiny. When the two statements are compared and adjustments made for expenses and taxes paid during the period, it is possible to compute the "taxable income not reported." For a simplified example, see the net worth statement reproduced here from the "Handbook for Special Agents."

The "expenditures method" is a variation

on the net worth method. According to the IRS, "The method is based on the theory that if the taxpayer's expenditures during a given year exceed reported income, and the source of such expenditures is unexplained, it may be inferred that such expenditures represent unreported income."

This method is used in preference to the net worth method whenever a taxpayer's assets did not change significantly during a taxable period. Generally, the expenditures method is effective against those taxpayers who "live it up" and do not accumulate much net worth.

Net worth statements are usually prepared as a backup to this method to counter a defendant's claim that assets were converted to cash to finance his lavish living.

The "bank deposits method" may be used if a taxpayer's books or records are not available to the investigators. At best, it is circumstantial evidence. This method is based on the assumption that "under certain circumstances proof of deposits is substantial evidence of taxable receipts."

The "certain circumstances" will generally be a taxpayer engaged in "a business or calling of a lucrative nature," who regularly and constantly deposits funds in a bank account and draws against them for his own use. Internal Revenue will show that the accused had an income-producing business, and then analyze and adjust the bank records to determine taxable income.

An alternate method is the "percentage method." Internal Revenue does not consider this a prime method and reminds agents it is "of very little value in criminal cases." However, this method of computing taxable income has been used successfully in civil cases.

Under the percentage method, taxable income is calculated using ratios or percentages "considered typical of the business under consideration." Approximations of sales, costs of sales, gross profit, or net profit can be

Exhibit 300-1

Net Worth Statement
Handbook Reference: Subsection 324.8

NET WORTH STATEMENT
John and Mary Roe
Dayton, Ohio

	ASSETS	12/31/	12/31/	12/31/
1.	Cash - First National Bank................	$ 4,200.00	$ 150.00	$ 2,500.00
2.	Cash on hand	25.00	25.00	25.00
3.	Inventory, Liquor Store..................	3,000.00	13,000.00	29,000.00
4.	U. S. Savings Bonds...................	-0-	3,750.00	-0-
5.	Note Receivable, Frank Roe	-0-	-0-	300.00
6.	Note Receivable, Roger Jones.........	-0-	-0-	16,000.00
7.	Accounts Receivable, Doc's Market.......	-0-	1,600.00	-0-
8.	Lot on Dayton Road	1,000.00	1,000.00	1,000.00
9.	Ohio Tourist Camp....................	12,000.00	12,000.00	12,000.00
10.	Residence, 1100 Vine Street............	2,300.00	2,300.00	-0-
11.	30 Acre Farm, East Dayton...........	-0-	7,400.00	7,400.00
12.	150 Acre Farm, North Dayton......	-0-	-0-	7,000.00
13.	Equipment - Liquor Store...............	800.00	800.00	800.00
14.	Ace Automobile	2,800.00	2,800.00	2,800.00
15.	Farm Truck.........................	-0-	-0-	300.00
16.	Farm Equipment......................	-0-	1,250.00	2,250.00
17.	Livestock on Farm...................	-0-	900.00	1,300.00
	Total Assets	$28,725.00	$47,475.00	$83,175.00
	LIABILITIES			
18.	First Federal Savings & Loan Assn.	$2,400.00	$ 1,800.00	$ -0-
19.	First National Bank	2,900.00	2,700.00	-0-
20.	Depreciation Reserve...............	2,500.00	3,200.00	4,300.00
	Total Liabilities	$7,800.00	$ 7,700.00	$ 4,300.00
	NET WORTH................	$20,925.00	$39,775.00	$78,875.00
	Less: Net Worth f Prior Year..........		20,925.00	39,775.00
	Increase in Net Worth.		$18,850.00	$39,100.00
	ADJUSTMENTS			
	Add:			
21.	Living Expenses		$ 2,500.00	$ 2,500.00
22.	Life Insurance Premium		300.00	500.00
23.	Federal Income Taxes Paid		750.00	900.00
	Less:			
24.	Long-Term Capital Gain on Sale of Residence (50%)......		-0-	(500.00)
25.	Inheritance		-0-	(10,000.00)
	Adjusted Gross Income................		$22,400.00	$32,500.00
	Less: Standard Deduction..........		1,000.00	1,000.00
	Balance		$21,400.00	$31,500.00
	Less: Exemptions (4).............		2,400.00	2,400.00
	Taxable Income		$19,000.00	$29,100.00
	Less: Taxable Income Reported		6,100.00	6,400.00
	Taxable Income Not Reported.............		$12,900.00	$22,700.00

Handbook for Special Agents

Exhibit 300-2

Expenditures Statement
Handbook Reference: Subsection 325.6

EXPENDITURES STATEMENT
John and Mary Roe
Dayton, Ohio

Item No.	Money Spent or Applied on Nondeductible Items	19__	19__
1.	Cash - First National Bank (increase)........	-0-	$ 2,350.00
3.	Inventories.................................	$ 8,200.00	16,000.00
4.	U. S. Savings Bonds........................	3,750.00	-0-
5.	Note Receivable, Frank Roe.................	-0-	300.00
6.	Note Receivable, Roger Jones...............	-0-	16,000.00
7.	Accounts Receivable, Doc's Market..........	1,600.00	-0-
11.	30 Acre Farm, East Dayton.................	7,400.00	-0-
12.	150 Acre Farm, North Dayton...............	-0-	7,000.00
15.	Farm Truck................................	-0-	800.00
16.	Farm Equipment...........................	1,250.00	1,000.00
17.	Livestock on Farm.........................	900.00	400.00
	Payments on Loan:		
18.	First Federal Savings & Loan Assn........	600.00	1,800.00
19.	First National Bank.....................	200.00	2,700.00
21.	Living Expense............................	2,500.00	2,500.00
22.	Life Insurance Premium....................	300.00	500.00
23.	Federal Income Taxes Paid.................	750.00	900.00
	TOTAL:	$27,450.00	$52,250.00

Nontaxable Sources of Funds

Item No.		19__	19__
1.	Cash - First National Bank (decrease)........	$ 4,350.00	-0-
4.	U. S. Saving Bonds.........................	-0-	$ 3,750.00
7.	Accounts Receivable, Doc's Market..........	-0-	1,600.00
10.	Sale of Residence, 1100 Vine Street (cost).....	-0-	2,800.00
20.	Depreciation reserve.......................	700.00	1,100.00
24.	Capital Gain on Sale of Residence,		
	1100 Vine Street (50%)...................	-0-	500.00
25.	Inheritance................................	-0-	10,000.00
	TOTAL:	$ 5,050.00	$19,750.00
	Adjusted Gross Income.....................	$22,400.00	$32,500.00
	Less: Standard Deduction................	1,000.00	1,000.00
	Balance...................................	$21,400.00	$31,500.00
	Less: Exemptions (4)....................	2,400.00	2,400.00
	Taxable Income............................	$19,000.00	$29,100.00
	Less: Taxable Income Reported	6,100.00	6,400.00
	Taxable Income Not Reported	$12,900.00	$22,700.00

made if some base figure can be found to be used as a starting point. As one possible example, the records of a business' suppliers could be combed to fix the costs of goods bought for resale, and other figures derived from this known one.

Rights of a Taxpayer

Taxpayers accused of criminal tax law violations have legal rights identical to those of any criminal defendant. These rights stem from the U.S. Constitution, but have been defined further by many court cases.

The Fifth Amendment provides that no one shall be compelled to be a witness against himself in a criminal case. Several precedents extend this right; it is legally allowed to refuse to answer incriminating questions in criminal proceedings. No presumption of guilt may arise from such refusal.

However, in dealing with Internal Revenue, there are restrictive interpretations of this right. A taxpayer cannot refuse to appear or to bring books and records when properly summoned by the IRS as part of a civil examination or audit; the taxpayer may refuse to testify or refuse to allow examination of the books and records on Fifth Amendment grounds, but he first must appear and bring the documents required.

A taxpayer may invoke this right at any stage of the proceedings, but whatever statements or records made available earlier (and not under protection of the Fifth Amendment) may be used as evidence against him.

As an example of the dangers inherent in interviews with IRS agents, here is the sort of statement an agent will read into the record to preface an interview with a taxpayer. (Variations of this are allowed; only the substance counts.)

"In connection with my investigation of your tax liability, I would like to ask you some questions. However, first I advise you that under the Fifth Amendment to the Constitution of the United States I cannot compel you to answer any questions or to submit any information if such answers or information might tend to incriminate you in any way. I also advise you that anything which you say and any documents which you submit may be used against you in any criminal proceeding which may be undertaken. I advise you further that you may, if you wish, seek the assistance of an attorney before responding."

Privilege does not apply to accountants. They may be required to testify as to their knowledge of their client's affairs. In addition, accountants' workpapers are generally considered to be their property, and may be subpoenaed by the IRS. Under certain circumstances, an accountant employed by an attorney, or by the taxpayer at the attorney's specific request, may be covered by the attorney-client privilege. The exact method of employment is very important; instruction by an experienced tax attorney before making this move is of overriding importance. Additionally, you cannot rely on information in the hands of your former accountant not being obtained by the IRS; obtaining physical possession of all your records at the outset of any criminal investigation may be advisable too.

A right of privilege is also assumed to exist between husband and wife, and neither is required to testify against the other, even by Internal Revenue. However, a recent Supreme Court ruling allows a spouse to voluntarily testify against the other.

Privilege is also assumed to exist between a doctor and a patient, or a clergyman and a penitent. IRS agents, though, have ready access to financial and other personal records, if not medical information, from physicians and hospitals.

In all cases, privilege generally does not extend to communications made in the presence of others not essential or party to the matter. If a secretary, a child old enough to understand, a friend, or anyone else is present when communicating a confidential matter to attorney or spouse, privilege may be destroyed.

If the taxpayer requests clarification of any point, an agent is required to explain. But, naturally, an explanation does not change the nature of the required statement. If a taxpayer declines to testify on Fifth Amendment grounds, the agent may not force him to do so. If a taxpayer testifies despite the warning given by the agent, he waives his legal rights, though he may still refuse later in the interview.

A taxpayer's right to legal counsel is provided for by the Sixth Amendment. This right applies when summoned to appear before special agents. It is perhaps the most important right, because an attorney will advise upon the other rights as necessary.

Communications between a taxpayer and his attorney are privileged under certain circumstances. This means that the attorney may not be required to testify about the taxpayer's affairs and allows free communication between them. This privilege is very important in criminal tax cases, because the attorney will be more effective if he knows the actual situation, the true extent of his client's guilt or involvement.

Note, though, that this privilege covers the client-attorney relationship only if the attorney is employed to give legal advice, represent the client in litigation, or perform some other function strictly as an attorney.

The client-attorney privilege does not apply in other circumstances. Communications are not privileged if the attorney simply handles funds or transfers real estate without any legal consultation, for example. If an individual acts as both attorney and accountant, privilege does not apply to communications made in relation to his auditing of books, or preparing a tax return for a client. (This is a very technical gray area, with some communications privileged and others not.)

What to Do?

After working through this chapter, the correct course of action if faced with criminal tax charges would be obvious.

At any point when it appears a criminal audit is underway, a taxpayer should immediately obtain a tax attorney. Even if an accountant has been working on the case, an attorney will be necessary. It may even be necessary, ruthless as it may seem, to discharge your current accountant or preparer, get back all your records that are in his hands, and have your new attorney engage any accounting help needed to prepare your defense.

The reason, of course, is that while a tax accountant is adequate for most civil involvement with the IRS, during a criminal audit it becomes another game, played to a different set of rules. More importantly, the stakes become higher. No longer is mere money involved; a taxpayer's freedom is at stake.

Consider the penalties provided for conviction under the criminal provisions of the Internal Revenue Code and the U.S. Code. They are as high as for such purely criminal acts as robbery, assault with a deadly weapon or manslaughter. Would you consider defending yourself against such charges without a lawyer?

It is hoped that readers of this manual will be faced only with civil problems when involved with the IRS, and never be investigated as a potential criminal tax violator. But if you ever are, you should get a good lawyer at your side, and quickly too.

Collecting the Money 10

The Internal Revenue Service has a reputation for playing rough. It has sometimes been called the "American Gestapo" because of the broad powers given its agents, and the activities of its revenue officers or "collectors."

If you have progressed this far in the manual, you know that there are several kinds of IRS agents, and that the functions of each are quite different.

The Collection Division, part of Internal Revenue's compliance arm, is charged with actually "getting the money." This is the IRS' essential function, so it is only to be expected that the Collection Division's Revenue Officers have been endowed with stronger powers than other IRS agents.

Tax auditor's revenue agents, and special agents all have the authority to issue summonses to a taxpayer, or to third parties, to compel them to appear, to produce records, and to testify. Special agents have limited powers of search and seizure too, pertaining mainly to records to be used as evidence. They can also arrest individuals charged with tax crimes.

Admittedly, these are heavy powers but revenue officers have been given even stronger tools. In addition to the right to issue summonses, they have been given the authority to seize and sell a taxpayer's property to satisfy a tax bill. There are various minor limitations, but basically, they may seize (i.e., levy) and sell any or all types of personal and real property: bank accounts, salary, monies due from others, furniture, vehicles, businesses, clothes, commercial real estate, the taxpayer's home, even more. Normally, this power is kept sheathed, but it is a foolish person indeed who does not cooperate with a revenue officer.

It is an even more foolish person who tries to run from them. With the powers described above, in this day of data banks and wide utilization of Social Security numbers as identification, it is not very difficult for a revenue officer to find and take what he wants, when he wants it, at least anywhere in the U.S.

Such seizures happen rarely, though. In 1975, for example, the collection division handled about 2.5 million delinquent accounts. Property was seized in only 18,000 cases, and only slightly more than 3,000 taxpayers had their property sold to pay their tax bills.

Much of Internal Revenue's bad publicity stems from the collection division's confrontations with just such foolish taxpayers. To intimidate potential tax violators, the IRS often releases news stories on convictions for tax fraud and the like. When revenue officers seize the property of a stubborn taxpayer, it is often unnecessary for the IRS to publicize the event. The taxpayer resists, a confrontation occurs, and the seizure becomes a big item in the local media.

These cases only arise because many taxpayers seemingly do not realize what happens if they are uncooperative with a revenue officer. They disregard Internal Revenue's collection letters, let past due taxes accumulate penalties and interest, or even refuse to pay. In such cases, the collection division is compelled to act.

Unfortunately, sometimes what seems to be a taxpayer's disregard of his obligations to the IRS is really a small business going through a bad period. Instances are numerous where economic cycles or industry-wide conditions, such as strikes, have temporarily prevented timely payment of employment or other taxes. Business taxpayers have been put out of business by Internal Revenue because of such communication gaps. If ever there was a situation where engagement of an imaginative tax advisor is important, the threat of a levy on business property is such a situation. There are ways out of such predicaments, but they are not common knowledge, and are not volunteered as solutions by the IRS. (Installment agreements and compromise offers are ways which will be covered later in this chapter.) Too often, the taxpayer learns of such procedures only after his assets have been sold at auction by a revenue officer.

An Important Difference

It is important for a taxpayer to make a distinction between Internal Revenue's examination division and its collection division. Many taxpayers who have a serious unpleasantness with collection seem not to understand the differences. There is a formal appeals process that allows a taxpayer to protest an auditor's proposed deficiency. If a taxpayer does not avail himself of this opportunity, or does not act within the prescribed time limits, the deficiency will be assessed as a tax due, and his case is routinely turned over

to the collection division for action. It is useless to go back and argue an assessment with the examination division once the collection process starts. The divisions operate independently; the collection process, once begun, is inexorable. A taxpayer trying to reopen a discussion with the auditing staff may well find his bank account seized by a revenue officer. The only effective way to continue to challenge the liability is to pay up and then file a refund claim to restart the appeals process.

The Collection Process

Taxpayer contact with IRS's collection division begins with a tax bill. A tax liability can be established by a service center, a district office, or by a decision in the appeals process. If the tax is not paid at the time an assessment is finalized, when a field or office audit is closed, for example, the collection process begins automatically.

The first step is simple—a bill for the tax due will be sent the taxpayer. This is both a notice and a demand; payment is required with 10 days. If the amount due is not paid within this 10-day period, the law gives Internal Revenue a "statutory lien" upon the taxpayer's property.

Inaction, even if a taxpayer believes the tax bill is incorrect or if he is unable to pay, will only complicate things unnecessarily.

Many tax bills are sent out by a service center, as we have seen. There is no formal appeals process for such notices. However, if the bill is wrong, a taxpayer should write the office sending the bill, or contact the nearest IRS branch office. This will initiate an examination of the return, perhaps a full audit, and delay the collection process until the matter is resolved.

If the bill cannot be paid within the prescribed 10 days, the taxpayer should contact his local Internal Revenue office to make payment arrangements.

Payment Arrangements

Internal Revenue is more than willing to make an arrangement to pay with a taxpayer who has not had an unpaid tax liability before. If a relatively short time is required to make full payment, detailed financial information from the taxpayer is not required. A short time is interpreted as "up to the next filing date or up to nine months from the date of an audit assessment."

An agreement may be reached, if the IRS is willing, to pay the tax, and any penalties and interest due, in installments (see Form 433-D); this usually requires a financial statement. Another possibility is to pay in one lump sum at a specified date (see Form 433-E).

If a taxpayer has previously owed taxes, the IRS holds out for much stricter terms.

Collection will first try to obtain immediate full payment, even if the taxpayer has no ready money with which to pay. The delinquent will be asked (required) to complete a "Collection Information Statement." Using this, a collection agent will review the taxpayer's financial status, with the objective of locating assets that can be converted to cash. The IRS will make suggestions, perhaps explaining how a second mortgage can be obtained on the taxpayer's home, or how an asset could be sold or used as collateral for a loan. If this financial review shows that he has the ability to pay the taxpayer is expected to act quickly, to come up with the cash to pay his tax bill. Naturally, a written agreement to pay will be extracted from the taxpayer.

If a previously delinquent taxpayer's financial condition is such that immediate, or rapid, full payment cannot be made, an installment agreement may be worked out. However, the IRS will not accept his estimate of the size of payments that he can make. Completion of yet another form is required; this one will dissect the taxpayer's monthly income and expenses. The collection agent will try to determine the maximum ability to pay. A payroll deduction arrangement, with payments made directly to Internal Revenue, may be required. Sometimes, a taxpayer is asked to provide a series of post-dated checks for deposit on specified dates. (This is a questionable procedure, since the inadvertent bouncing of a check on the IRS can result in both a specific penalty, and sour the working relationship with the Collection Division for the future.) The taxpayer must agree to remain current on future taxes and to make all payments on time. In some cases, the IRS will monitor the taxpayer's affairs by requiring periodic financial reviews.

Delayed Collection

Sometimes, in special cases and in its own interest, the IRS will suspend collection proceedings temporarily. Interest and penalties will continue to pile up, but the taxpayer will be given time to get back on his financial feet.

Such a course is not likely to be taken if the taxpayer has any significant assets or a current income flow; the IRS will take its share of these as we have just outlined.

As an example, consider a writer who owes perhaps $20,000 to the IRS, but is basically broke. Yet his earning prospects remain high. Perhaps he is working on a book for which he will receive a $50,000 advance. Ever sensible in such a case, Internal Revenue will often wait and take their $20,000, plus interest and penalties, from the writer's future income. Collection prospects will undoubtedly be insured by a levy filed with the writer's publishers; the taxes due will pass directly from the publishing firm to the IRS.

Offer in Compromise

A taxpayer in debt to Uncle Sam also has the right to make an "offer in compromise" to the IRS. The Commissioner of Internal Revenue has the authority to compromise, to

Form **433-D** (Rev June 1978)	Department of the Treasury — Internal Revenue Service **Installment Agreement**

Names and Address of Taxpayer(s)	Social Security or Employer Identification Number	
	Kinds of Taxes *(Form numbers)*	Check *(As appropriate)*
	Tax Periods	☐ Individual ☐ Corporation
	Amount of Tax Owed	☐ Partnership

The undersigned agrees that the Federal taxes shown above, plus any interest and penalties provided by law, will be paid as follows:

$ _____ to be paid on _____ and $ _____ to be paid on the _____ of each _____ thereafter until the liability is paid in full and also agrees that the above tax installments will be increased as follows:

Date of Increase					
Amount of Increase	$				
New Installment Amount	$				

Conditions of This Agreement:
- All Federal taxes that become due during the term of this agreement will be paid on time.
- All Federal tax returns that become due during the term of this agreement will be filed on time.
- Until this liability is satisfied, any refunds that might otherwise be due will be applied to this liability.
- If the conditions of this agreement are not met, or if it is determined that collection of these taxes is endangered, permission to make installment payments may be withdrawn, and the entire tax liability may be collected by levy on income or by seizure of property.

Additional Conditions:

Your Signature	Title *(If corporate officer or partner)*	Date	For Assistance, Contact
Spouse's Signature *(If joint income tax return)*		Date	Telephone:
Agreement Examined and Approved by *(Signature)*		Date	Interviewer

Note: When making an installment payment, please be sure to:

1. Write your social security or employer identification number on each payment.

2. Make each payment in an amount at least equal to that specified in this agreement. For example do not double one payment and skip the next without contacting us.

3. Enclose with each payment a copy of the reminder notice (if you received one), in the envelope provided.

4. Mail your payment on time to the proper IRS office, even if you did not receive a reminder notice.

5. Contact us immediately if you cannot meet the terms of this agreement.

Part 2 — Taxpayer's Copy   Form 433-D (Rev. 6-78)

Form **433-E**	Department of the Treasury — Internal Revenue Service			
(Rev. March 1977)	**Payment Agreement**			
	(If more space is needed, please use back of form)			

Name of Taxpayer		Home Phone	Payment Due Date	Payment Amount

I request permission and agree to pay the amount of Federal taxes I owe (including penalty and interest) by the date due as shown above. I understand that any refunds due me will be applied against my liability until it is satisfied. I also understand that if I fail to pay as agreed, my tax liability may be collected by levy on my income or by seizure of my property.

Taxpayer's Signature	Taxpayer's Identifying Number	Date	Interviewer's Initials	Approving Official's Initials

Taxpayer's Employer *(Name and address)*		Phone Number	Take-Home Pay	Paydays

Spouse's Employer *(Name and address)*		Phone Number	Take-Home Pay	Paydays

Bank Accounts *(Names and addresses of banks)*	Motor Vehicles *(Description and license number of each vehicle you own)*
	Real Property *(Location, description, equity, and mortgage holder)*

Part 1—Office Copy   Form 433—E (Rev. 3-77)

Form **656** (Rev. June 1978)	Department of the Treasury - Internal Revenue Service **Offer in Compromise**	To Be Filed in Duplicate

Names and Address of Taxpayers	For Office Use Only	

Offer is - *(Check applicable box)*

☐ Cash *(Paid in full)*

☐ Deferred payment

Serial Number

(Cashier's stamp)

Social Security and Employer
Identification Numbers

To: **Commissioner of Internal Revenue**   Date   Amount Paid $

1. This offer is submitted by the undersigned proponents (persons making this offer) to compromise a liability resulting from alleged violations of law or failure to pay an internal revenue liability as follows: _____

(State specifically the alleged violation involved, the kind of unpaid tax liability, and each period involved)

2. The total sum of $ _____ paid in full or payable on a deferred payment basis as follows: [1]

with interest at the annual rate as established under section 6621(a) of the Internal Revenue Code (subject to adjustments as provided by Code section 6621(b)) on the deferred payments, if any, from the date the offer is accepted until it is paid in full, is voluntarily tendered with this offer with the request that it be accepted to compromise the liability described above, and any statutory additions to this liability.

3. In making this offer, and as a part of the consideration, it is agreed (a) that the United States shall keep all payments and other credits made to the accounts for the periods covered by this offer, and (b) that the United States shall keep any and all amounts to which the taxpayer—proponents may be entitled under the internal revenue laws, due through overpayments of any tax or other liability, including interest and penalties, for periods ending before or within or as of the end of the calendar year in which this offer is accepted (and which are not in excess of the difference between the liability sought to be compromised and the amount offered). Any such refund received after this offer is filed will be returned immediately.

4. It is also agreed that payments made under the terms of this offer shall be applied first to tax and penalty, in that order, due for the earliest taxable period, then to tax and penalty, in that order, for each succeeding taxable period with no amount to be allocated to interest until the liabilities for taxes and penalties for all taxable periods sought to be compromised have been satisfied.

5. It is further agreed that upon notice to the taxpayers of the acceptance of this offer, the taxpayers shall have no right to contest in court or otherwise the amount of the liability sought to be compromised; and that if this is a deferred payment offer and there is a default in payment of any installment of principal or interest due under its terms, the United States, at the option of the Commissioner of Internal Revenue or a delegated official, may (a) proceed immediately by suit to collect the entire unpaid balance of the offer; or (b) proceed immediately by suit to collect as liquidated damages an amount equal to the liability sought to be compromised, minus any deposits already received under the terms of the offer, with interest on the unpaid balance at the annual rate as established under section 6621(a) of the Internal Revenue Code (subject to adjustments as provided by Code section 6621 (b)) from the date of default; or (c) disregard the amount of the offer and apply all amounts previously deposited under the offer against the amount of the liability sought to be compromised and, without further notice of any kind, assess and collect by levy or suit the balance of the liability, the right of appeal to the United States Tax Court and the restrictions against assessment and collection

being waived upon acceptance of this offer.

6. The taxpayer—proponents waive the benefit of any statute of limitations applicable to the assessment and collection of the liability sought to be compromised, and agree to the suspension of the running of the statutory period of limitations on assessment and collection for the period during which this offer is pending, or the period during which any installment remains unpaid, and for 1 year thereafter.

7. The following facts and reasons are submitted as grounds for acceptance of this offer: _____
_____
_____
_____

(If space is insufficient, please attach a supporting statement)

8. It is understood that this offer will be considered and acted upon in due course and that it does not relieve the taxpayers from the liability sought to be compromised unless and until the offer is accepted in writing by the Commissioner or a delegated official, and there has been full compliance with the terms of the offer.

[1] *If this offer is paid in full at the time it is filed, show in item 2 the amount only. If this is a deferred payment offer, show (a) the amount deposited at the time of filing this offer; (b) any amount deposited on prior offers which are applied on this offer; (c) the amount of each deferred payment, and the date on which each payment is to be made. (Amounts payable after the filing date of the offer, including amounts payable upon notice of acceptance, are deferred payments.)*

I accept the waiver of statutory period of limitations for the Internal Revenue Service.	Under penalties of perjury, I declare that I have examined this offer, including accompanying schedules and statements, and to the best of my knowledge and belief it is true, correct, and complete.
Signature	Signature of Proponent
Title Date	Signature of Proponent

Form **656** (Rev. 6-78)

For Office Use Only

Liability Incurred By *(List taxpayers included under same account no.)*   Kind of Liability *(Complete description)*

Date Notice of Lien Filed   Place Notice of Lien Filed   Was Bond Filed? *(If yes, attach copy)* ☐ Yes ☐ No

Were Assets Pledged as Security? *(If yes, attach complete information)* ☐ Yes ☐ No   Periods Involved and Dates Returns Filed for Offers Involving Delinquency Penalties Only   Were Tax Collection Waivers Filed? *(If yes, attach copies)* ☐ Yes ☐ No

Attach Transcript of Accounts

accept a lesser amount in full payment of the tax bill.

Such a compromise can only be made if there is a substantial doubt as to the validity of the tax liability, or if there is just no way the full amount can be paid.

A compromise offer might be accepted during the appeals process, as an out-of-court settlement, if the IRS doubts both that the courts will decide in its favor, and that the taxpayer can pay.

Compromises can also be made if the taxpayer is in financial trouble, not necessarily on the verge of bankruptcy, but with no reasonable expectations of being able to pay the full amount in the near future. Even then, to have a compromise offer considered, the taxpayer must offer an amount in excess of the total value of his equity in all his assets. Basically, if the compromise offer is accepted, the IRS will settle for less but take everything the taxpayer has, rather than force the taxpayer into bankruptcy because of debts owned other creditors. Sometimes, a family member of a friend might be willing to make a loan to help the situation, provided the IRS cooperates with an "offer in compromise." But don't do this in reverse order—borrowing, then trying to compromise; Internal Revenue will take the loan proceeds and then talk compromise.

For the reader's consideration, a copy of Form 656, "Offer in Compromise," is provided here. The services of a tax representative would seem necessary if collection proceedings ever progressed to the stage where an "offer in compromise" were needed.

Enforced Collection

In all of the above types of payment arrangements, Internal Revenue's agreement is contingent on taxpayer cooperation. If an individual owing taxes does not contact the IRS, or makes an agreement but does not follow through with regular payments, the collection division will take direct action to insure payment.

Internal Revenue's collection division is the envy of repossessors and finance companies everywhere. The reason, of course, is the IRS's spectacular powers to enforce payment without relying on the courts.

Internal Revenue uses mainly liens, levies, and seizures to force payment from negligent or uncooperative taxpayers.

Federal Tax Liens

A statutory tax lien automatically exists once a tax bill remains unpaid for more than the allowable 10 days. However, at this stage the tax lien is merely a legal concept, a pending threat to the taxpayer's financial future.

Internal Revenue may decide, though, to formally file a "Notice of Federal Tax Lien." This is done with an appropriate state court to create a public record. It serves notice to all concerned that the federal government has an enforceable claim against the delinquent's assets, now and in the future.

A "Notice of Federal Tax Lien" will generally affect a taxpayer's credit rating, the lien will act as a warning flag to banks and other lenders until such time as it is removed by the IRS.

Internal Revenue may occasionally file a lien against a taxpayer already paying on an installment agreement, or when collections have been delayed by arrangement, to insure payment of the tax bill.

Once filed, a "Notice of Federal Tax Lien" will not be released until full payment is made. All fees charged by the state for filing and release of the lien are added to the taxpayer's bill.

Levies

The most effective and most used enforcement tool is a levy. It is a simple form, filled

Form **668-A**
(Rev. December, 1978)

Department of the Treasury—Internal Revenue Service

Notice of Levy

To

Date

Originating District

The taxpayer named at the bottom of this notice
owes the United States ▶ $

Kind of Tax	Tax Period Ended	Date of Assessment	Identifying Number	Unpaid Balance of Assessment	Statutory Additions	Total
				$	$	$

Total amount due ▶ $

Chapter 64 of the Internal Revenue Code provides a lien for the above tax and statutory additions.   Demand has been made on the taxpayer for the above amount. The taxpayer has neglected or refused to pay. The amount is still due, owing, and unpaid. All property, rights to property, money, credits, and bank deposits now in your possession and belonging to this taxpayer (or for which you are obligated) and all money or other obligations owing from you to this taxpayer, are levied upon for payment of the tax plus all additions provided by law. Demand is made on you for the amount necessary to pay this tax liability or for any smaller sum that you owe this taxpayer, to be applied as a payment on this tax liability. Checks or money orders should be made payable to the Internal Revenue Service.

Signature

Title

Name and Office Address

Name and Address of Taxpayer

Certificate of Service

I certify that this notice of levy was served by delivering a copy of it to the person named below.

Name

Title

Date and Time

Signature of Revenue Officer or Service Representative

Part 1—To be returned to Internal Revenue Service   Form 668-A (Rev. 12-78) out and signed by a revenue agent, that allows him to take property belonging to a taxpayer to satisfy the tax bill. No court approval is needed for a levy.

Levies may be served on any or all parties believed to have money or other valuables belonging to the taxpayer. A bank, an employer, anyone owing money to the delinquent taxpayer, has no choice but to give the IRS what it wants. Form 668-A, "Notice of Levy," (reproduced here) states: All property, rights to property, money, credits, and bank deposits now in your possession and belonging to this taxpayer (or for which you are obligated) and all money or other obligations owing from you to this taxpayer, are levied upon for payment of the tax. . . .Demand is made upon you for the amount necessary to pay this tax liability or for any smaller sum that you owe this taxpayer. . ."

Those upon whom a levy is served are personally liable for payment. If remittance to the IRS is not made freely, it will be taken anyway by "judicial process," with interest and a penalty of 50 percent added. Payment of an IRS levy legally relieves the third party of his obligations to the delinquent taxpayer. As a result of such laws, an IRS levy is almost never ignored.

Banks are notoriously shy when it comes to "Notices of Levy." They have been known to provide revenue officers with business names in which taxpayers have made deposits, and generally to be overly helpful to the IRS. A levy on a bank account, if larger than the balance in the account, will effectively liquidate it. Every cent goes to the IRS, as well as all deposits made after the levy is received. Checks drawn on the account will not be honored and will bounce until the levy is satisfied. Levies on salaries or on accounts receivable will effectively cut off funds from these sources, in most cases.

From these simple examples it can be seen that the levy is a powerful tool. Once Internal Revenue resorts to a levy, a taxpayer has little choice but to give in and pay up, if he is still able to.

Certain property is exempt from levy. The full list is in fine print on the reverse of IRS Form 668-B, illustrated here. (This form is the primary one, the one given or sent to a taxpayer.) The exemptions include wearing apparel and school books, some personal effects, tools used in a trade or business, and income of $50 per week plus $15 for each dependent.

As a matter of policy, Internal Revenue has expanded these exemptions. It does not, for example, normally take Social Security, Medicare, or workmen's compensation payments, even though they are not exempt. The law allows only $500 of exempt personal effects and $250 of business and professional tools; the IRS usually exempts $1,500 of household property and $1,000 of business property. Only in flagrant cases of refusal to pay will it go after this type of property.

Seizures and Sales

A seizure is just a levy against more substantial types of personal and real property. Internal Revenue normally takes the more liquid and obtainable resources held by third parties first. Only if these are insufficient to satisfy the tax liability will it move to seize vehicles, furniture, businesses, or real estate. One practical consideration is that this type of property must be sold before any monies are realized. Another factor is that often permission must first be obtained from a court to enter private premises to get at the property.

But if it must resort to seizure and sale, it will. Perishable property seized will be sold quickly to avoid spoilage. Otherwise, at least 10 days' notice is given the taxpayer and the public before a sale of seized property. In cities where there is a district office, newspaper notices of IRS auctions of seized property are common.

Form 668-B
(Rev. December 1978)

Department of the Treasury - Internal Revenue Service

Levy

Due from

Originating Internal Revenue District (*City and State*)

Kind of tax	Tax period ended	Date of assessment	Identifying number	Unpaid balance of assessment	Statutory Additions	Total
				$	$	$

Total Amount Due ▶

The amounts shown above are now due, owing, and unpaid to the United States from the above taxpayer for internal revenue taxes. Notice and demand have been made for payment. Chapter 64 of the Internal Revenue Code provides a lien for the above tax and statutory additions. Section 6331 of the Code authorizes collection of taxes by levy on all property or rights to property of a taxpayer, except property that is exempt under Code section 6334. Therefore, under the provisions of Code section 6331, so much of the property or rights to property, either real or personal, as may be necessary to pay the unpaid balance of assessment shown, with additions provided by law, including fees, costs, and expenses of this levy, are levied on to pay the taxes and additions.

_____ was asked to be present during inventory. _____
Taxpayer's Name   Revenue Officer Signature

_____ was present at inventory. ☐ Yes ☐ No
Taxpayer or Taxpayer's Representative's Name

Dated at _____ this _____ day of _____, 19___

Signature   Title

Applicable Sections Under The Internal Revenue Code

SEC. 6321.   Lien for Taxes
SEC. 6322.   Period of Lien
SEC. 6323.   Validity and Priority Against Certain Persons
SEC. 6324.   Special Liens for Estate and Gift Taxes
SEC. 6325.   Release of Lien or Discharge of Property
SEC. 6331.   Levy and Distraint
SEC. 6332.   Surrender of Property Subject to Levy
SEC. 6334.   Property Exempt from Levy
SEC. 6335.   Sale of Seized Property
SEC. 6339.   Legal Effect of Certificate of Sale of Personal Property and Deed of Real Property
SEC. 6343.   Authority to Release Levy and Return Property

SEC. 6331.   Levy and Distraint

(a) **Authority of Secretary.** — If any person liable to pay any tax neglects or refuses to pay the same within 10 days after notice and demand, it shall be lawful for the Secretary to collect such tax (and such further sum as shall be sufficient to cover the expenses of the levy) by levy upon all property and rights to property (except such property as is exempt under section 6334) belonging to such person or on which there is a lien provided in this chapter for the payment of such tax. Levy may be made upon the accrued salary or wages of any officer, employee, or elected official, of the United States, the District of Columbia, or any agency or instrumentality of the United States or the District of Columbia, by serving a notice of levy on the employer (as defined in section 3401 (d)) of such officer, employee, or elected official. If the Secretary makes a finding that the collection of such tax is in jeopardy, notice and demand for immediate payment of such tax may be made by the Secretary and, upon failure or refusal to pay such tax, collection thereof by levy shall be lawful without regard to the 10-day period provided in this section.

(b) **Seizure and Sale of Property.** — The term "levy" as used in this title includes the power of distraint and seizure by any means. *Except as otherwise provided in subsection* (d) (3), *a levy* shall extend only to property possessed and obligations existing at the time thereof. In any case in which the Secretary may levy upon property or rights to property, he may seize and sell such property or rights to property (whether real or personal, tangible or intangible).

(c) **Successive Seizures.** — Whenever any property or right to property upon which levy has been made by virtue of subsection (a) is not sufficient to satisfy the claim of the United States for which levy is made, the Secretary may, thereafter, and as often as may be necessary, proceed to levy in like manner upon any other property liable to levy of the person against whom such claim exists, until the amount due from him, together with all expenses, is fully paid.

SEC. 6332.   Surrender of Property Subject to Levy.

(a) **Requirement.** — Except as otherwise provided in subsection (b), any person in possession of (or obligated with respect to) property or rights to property subject to levy upon which a levy has been made shall, upon demand of the Secretary, surrender such property or rights (or discharge such obligation) to the Secretary, except such part of the property or rights as is, at the time of such demand, subject to an attachment or execution under any judicial process.

(c) **Enforcement of Levy.**

(1) **Extent of Personal Liability.** — Any person who fails or refuses to surrender any property or rights to property, subject to levy, upon demand by the Secretary, shall be liable in his own person and estate to the United States in a sum equal to the value of the property or rights not so surrendered, but not exceeding the amount of taxes for the collection of which such levy has been made, together with costs and interest on such sum at an annual rate established under section 6621 from the date of such levy (or, in the case of a levy described in section 6331 (d) (3), from the date such person would otherwise have been obligated to pay over such amounts to the taxpayer). Any amount (other than costs) recovered under this paragraph shall be credited against the tax liability for the collection of which such levy was made.

(2) **Penalty for Violation.** — In addition to the personal liability imposed by paragraph (1), if any person required to surrender property or rights to property fails or refuses to surrender such property or rights to property without reasonable cause, such person shall be liable for a penalty equal to 50 percent of the amount recoverable under paragraph (1). No part of such penalty shall be credited against the tax liability for the collection of which such levy was made.

(d) **Effect of Honoring Levy.** — Any person in possession of (or obligated with respect to) property or rights to property subject to levy upon which a levy has been made who, upon demand by the Secretary, surrenders such property or rights to property (or discharges such obligation) to the Secretary (or who pays a liability under subsection (c)(1) shall be discharged from any obligation or liability to the delinquent taxpayer with respect to such property or rights to property arising from such surrender payment. In the case of a levy which is satisfied pursuant to subsection (b), such organization shall also be discharged from any obligation or liability to any beneficiary arising from such surrender or payment.

(e) **Person Defined.** — The term "person," as used in subsection (a), includes an officer or employee of a corporation or a member or employee of a partnership, who as such officer, employee, or member is under a duty to surrender the property or rights to property, or to discharge the obligation.

SEC. 6334.   Property Exempt from Levy

(a) **Enumeration.** — There shall be exempt from levy —

(1) **Wearing Apparel and School Books.** — Such items of wearing apparel and such school books as are necessary for the taxpayer or for members of his family;

(2) **Fuel, Provisions, Furniture, and Personal Effects.** — If the taxpayer is the head of a family, so much of the fuel, provisions, furniture, and personal effects in his household, and of the arms for personal use, livestock, and poultry of the taxpayer, as does not exceed $500 in value;

(3) **Books and Tools of a Trade, Business, or Profession.** — So many of the books and tools necessary for the trade, business, or profession of the taxpayer as do not exceed in the aggregate $250 in value.

(4) **Unemployment Benefits.** — Any amount payable to an individual with respect to his unemployment (including any portion thereof payable with respect to dependents) under an unemployment compensation law of the United States, of any State, or of the District of Columbia or of the Commonwealth of Puerto Rico.

(5) **Undelivered Mail.** — Mail, addressed to any person, which has not been delivered to the addressee.

(6) **Certain Annuity and Pension Payments.** — Annuity or pension payments under the Railroad Retirement Act, benefits under the Railroad Unemployment Insurance Act, special pension payments received by a person whose name has been entered on the Army, Navy, Air Force, and Coast Guard Medal of Honor roll (38 U.S.C. 562), and annuities based on retired or retainer pay under chapter 73 of title 10 of the United States Code.

(7) **Workmen's Compensation.** — Any amount payable to an individual as workmen's compensation (including any portion thereof payable with respect to dependents) under a workmen's compensation law of the United States, any State, the District of Columbia, or the Commonwealth of Puerto Rico.

(8) **Judgments for Support of Minor Children.** — If the taxpayer is required by judgment of a court of competent jurisdiction, entered prior to the date of levy, to contribute to the support of his minor children, so much of his salary, wages, or other income as is necessary to comply with such judgment.

(9) **Minimum Exemption for Wages, Salary, and other Income.** — Any amount payable to or received by an individual as wages or salary for personal services, or as income derived from other sources, during any period, to the extent that the total of such amounts payable to or received by him during such period does not exceed the applicable exempt amount determined under subsection (d).

SEC. 6343.   Authority to Release Levy and Return Property

(a) **Release of Levy.** — It shall be lawful for the Secretary, under regulations prescribed by the Secretary, to release the levy upon all or part of the property or rights to property levied upon where the Secretary determines that such action will facilitate the collection of the liability, but such release shall not operate to prevent any subsequent levy.

Proceeds from the sale of confiscated goods are applied first to the costs of the levy and sale, and then to the tax bill. Any balance remaining on the tax bill may result in further seizures.

A taxpayer has the right to redeem his property before sale. To do this, he must pay the complete tax bill, plus the expenses of the seizure. Real estate can be redeemed by the taxpayer even after it is sold, at least for 120 days, by reimbursing the purchaser the amount paid the IRS, plus interest at 20 percent per year.

Points to Consider

Obviously, a taxpayer should try to avoid letting his tax affairs deteriorate to the state where IRS' collection division becomes in-volved. Sometimes of course, this ideal is impossible; an audit may result in an assessment so large it creates a cash bind.

To stall a revenue agent or a tax auditor is often an effective tactic. To stall a revenue officer or worse still, flee the particular jurisdiction, is bad judgment. The collection division is interested in only one thing—getting the money due the government. Excuses, delays, or provocations are likely to be met with a levy.

Once a levy is applied, your cash flow will be cut off. And the effect of this on your affairs will often be much costlier than the money involved.

Be careful with the collection division. It is far better to seek funds elsewhere temporarily than to challenge collection.

Appeal Within the IRS 11

If a taxpayer does not agree with an IRS auditor's proposed assessment, there are both informal and formal appeal routes.

Informally, a tax auditor's assessment can be immediately talked over with his supervisor, as discussed in Chapter 6. If a taxpayer does not agree with a revenue agent's proposal after a field audit, an informal appeal can be made to his group manager. A phone call is enough to set this up. It is recommended that this informal effort not be skipped; these are the individuals who are the first line of review above the auditor.

Don't think that you will upset things if you take this step. On the other hand, if everything has been resolved in a relatively favorable manner, don't run the risk of having things recalculated or renegotiated, especially if you have established a principle in your favor that can be used in future years.

Formal Appeal

Past this point, a taxpayer enters the formal tax appeal system. His effort to adjust IRS' assessment can be taken to higher levels of Internal Revenue, or outside the IRS, through several levels of courts, perhaps even to the U.S. Supreme Court itself, if it will take the case which, admittedly, would be rare.

Administrative Appeal

Most practical, because it is quicker, simpler and cheaper, is the appeals system run by the IRS itself.

It is to Internal Revenue's advantage to resolve a case quickly, without recourse to litigation. With this in mind, in 1978 the IRS streamlined its appeals process. Two levels of internal appeal were consolidated into one, at regional level.

Each region now has its Regional Director of Appeals, responsible for all taxpayer appeals in his jurisdiction. Under his jurisdiction are a group of "conferees."

Proceedings at this level are informal; the actual meeting with the taxpayer is called a "conference." The IRS is represented by a "conferee"; the taxpayer may present his own case, or be accompanied or represented by a tax advisor. The taxpayer's representative must be a lawyer, a CPA, or someone "enrolled to practice before the IRS." A signed power-of-attorney (usually Form 2848) must be filed for this representative. In the interest of simplicity, no transcript is made of the conference proceedings.

Internal Revenue takes the position that a taxpayer who disagrees with a proposed change in tax liability "is entitled to a prompt, *independent* review of the case." (Editor's emphasis.)

Despite this, the conferee is not a truly disinterested, independent party. He is an IRS employee whose job it is to get the taxpayer to agree to as much of the proposed assessment as possible and yet, to try to resolve the matter so that it goes no further.

It has been said that the internal appeals process is backwards; the agent who knows the facts best settles on the basis of legal issues, and the conferee, more often than not settles on the basis of facts to which he has no direct access. The conferee works primarily from the auditor's report, the revenue agent's report (the "RAR" to practitioners). The burden of proof remains upon the taxpayer, as it did in the audit. (But the taxpayer, with access to the RAR, now has the advantage of knowing what his adversary will attempt to establish.) He may present whatever evidence is deemed necessary to convince the conferee of his case: Documents, affidavits from third parties, even witnesses. If the agent has omitted or misrepresented the facts on the RAR, an alert tax representative has an opportunity to demolish factually the auditor's report. Usually, the conferee will be reluctant to have the agent redo his work, although he may consult with him later about the quality of his product.

The major advantages of the appeals conference to the taxpayer are the conferee's experience and his desire to eliminate unnecessary appeals to the courts and to settle cases because of the "hazards of litigation" on a percentage or issue-swapping basis. As a rule, conferees have had many years of duty either as auditors or as Appellate Division personnel. (Appellate Division was the former name of the Appeals Division.) They are likely to be more objective, canny, and decisive both because of their experience, and because the agent who performed the audit will not be present.

The conferee will try to come to an agreement on the assessment with the taxpayer. If an agreement is reached, the taxpayer will be asked to sign waiver Form 870. If a mutually acceptable assessment cannot be worked out,

the conferee will advise the taxpayer of his additional appeal rights.

Arranging a Conference

A taxpayer's request for a conference must be made within the period allowed by IRS' "Preliminary Notice," the "30-day letter." If he waits until he receives a "90-day letter," it is too late. A conference will then no longer be possible; the taxpayer must either pay the tax or take his case to the U.S. Tax Court.

The request for an appeals conference is directed to the local district office, who will forward it (with the case jacket) to the regional appeals office for action. This unit will arrange a mutually convenient time and place for the conference with the taxpayer.

Such a request can be made informally by the taxpayer in three situations:

1. If the examination was conducted by correspondence (a "limited contact" audit);
2. If the audit was conducted at an IRS office (a "desk" audit); or
3. If the assessment resulting from a field audit "does not exceed $2,500 for any of the periods involved."

Protests

If more than $2,500 is involved, a formal, written "protest" must be filed with the district director, again within the allowed 30 days. Instructions for this written protest are contained in the material that accompanies the 30-day letter.

Specifically, the protest should contain:

" 1. A statement that you want to appeal the findings of the examining officer to the Regional Director of Appeals;
2. Your name and address;
3. The date and symbols from the letter

transmitting the proposed adjustments and findings you are protesting;

4. The tax periods or years involved;

5. An itemized schedule of the adjustments with which you do not agree;

6. A statement of facts supporting your position in any contested factual issues; and

7. A statement outlining the law or other authority upon which you rely."

Statement (5) presents an interesting choice to the taxpayer and his advisor. Some professionals feel the chance of success at conference level is enhanced if minor issues are conceded and the protest limited to major issues of controversy. Sometimes, though, a taxpayer might want to include issues that he is willing to concede just to have something to trade at conference time.

At this appeals level, it is wasted effort to protest issues on the IRS "appeals coordinated issues" list. These issues are matters on which the IRS, as a matter of defensive policy, will not compromise. The only hope in such cases is to appeal through the courts. Even then, Internal Revenue will marshall its legal talent and fight to the legal end.

Contesting such issues is guaranteed to be expensive. By far the best tactic where an issue on this list is concerned is to arrange your affairs so that you will not butt heads with the IRS. Any tax professional should be cognizant of the problem areas on Internal Revenue's "appeals coordinated issues" list, even though the IRS is semi-secretive about its contents.

Statement (6) is the key to most successful protests. The advantage will be with the taxpayer if he can overcome the factual findings of the agent in the RAR. But the taxpayer must remember that "facts are facts," and cannot be constructed out of "whole cloth." Statement (6) must be "declared true under penalties of perjury," with the following

declaration added to the end of the protest letter and signed by the taxpayer.

"Under the penalties of perjury, I declare that I have examined the statement of facts presented in this protest and in any accompanying schedules and statements and, to the best of my knowledge and belief, they are true correct, and complete."

If a taxpayer's representative submits the protest, a modified form of declaration is used.

A protest letter presents the most difficult technical problem in using the appeals conference method. Even a taxpayer who can compose a beautiful bureaucratic communication will have difficulty with item (7). Content is the problem; the ability to organize your case and to write a proper letter is not enough. It is a rare taxpayer who, on his own, can produce the necessary factual statement and the persuasive legal argument necessary to a successful protest letter. Professional advice is essential for most taxpayers.

The Research Task

In statement (7), the taxpayer or his advisor must quote chapter and verse of "the law or other authority upon which" the appeal is based. Research into the necessary sources is a time-consuming task; it is doubtful if 30 days is enough unless the researcher has a tax library at hand and knows how to use it.

Among the normal sources are the tax laws and their amendments, Treasury and IRS regulations, revenue rulings, court decisions, IRS "acquiescences" and "non-acquiescences," and expressions of "legislative intent."

The complexity of the research job might overwhelm even the most pendantic and careful individual. The Internal Revenue code now runs to thousands of pages, and is constantly being amended and added to by Congress. Every effort is made to qualify, to cover every contingency, before Congress passes a tax bill. Sometimes the law is not clear enough, and the question of "legislative intent" arises. It is then necessary to go back to the *Congressional Record* or to congressional committee reports to determine what Congress had in mind when they drafted the law.

IRS regulations are "administrative law" with the force and effect of law to a conferee. They are Internal Revenue's interpretation of and instructions on the tax laws issuing from Congress. They are the IRS' internal law. Consequently, if a regulation is against you, an appeal to the IRS will always be decided against you. The only recourse is to the courts, which, if the regulation has been in force for a number of years, will normally rule for the IRS.

"Revenue rulings" are issued by the IRS often in response to specific written taxpayer requests for private rulings, and sometimes upon request of a district office for technical advice. They are Internal Revenue's interpretations of specific questions of tax law. Sometimes, if the questions and answers are considered pertinent to many taxpayers, revenue rulings are published.

An "acquiescence" is an agreement by the IRS with a Tax Court decision in a case it has lost. Generally, the IRS will not contest future cases involving the same issue.

A "non-acquiescence" means the IRS will not accept the precedent in future cases; when a similar issue is being fought the IRS will litigate in the hopes another judge will rule in its favor. Such IRS reactions to various court decisions in tax cases are published in the "Internal Revenue Bulletin."

There are not many taxpayers who can handle such research, especially within the time limitations prescribed for a protest letter. Even the exact form of citation used in the protest letter is very important. The conferee will deprecate any argument that does not follow the customary bureaucratic-legal format. It would generally seem to be a better idea to let a qualified professional handle the chore when a protest is necessary.

A Taxpayer's Chances

In 1978, the appeals division completed 31,904 cases, one way or another. Agreement was reached in 22,098 or 71 percent of these. In many agreed cases the assessment, though not eliminated entirely, was reduced by the conferee. Of the remainder, in some instances the taxpayer defaulted, letting his statutory time run out. Still others went on to other appeal levels, primarily the U.S. Tax Court.

For an overview of the appeals process, the reader is referred to the illustration that follows.

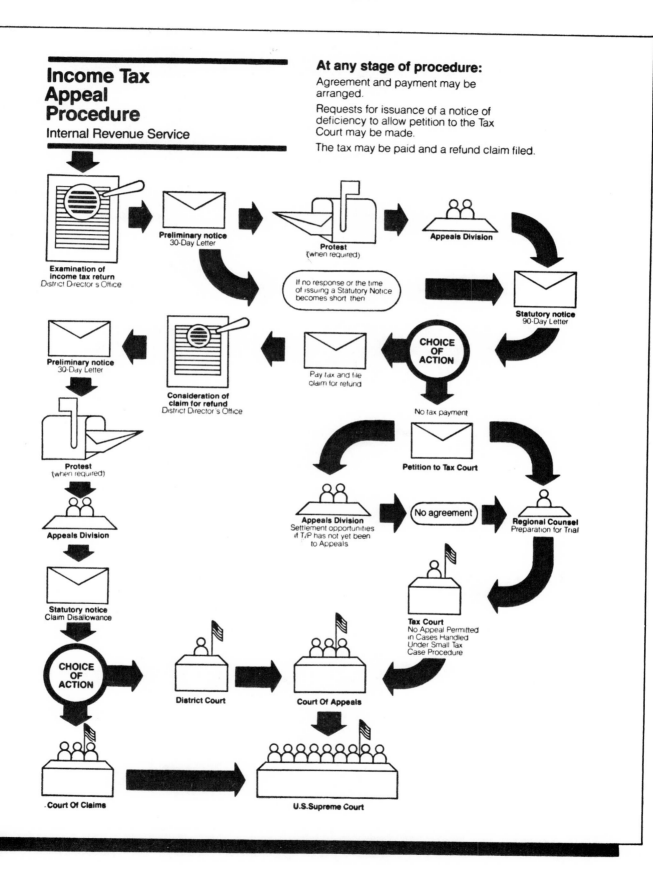

Income Tax Appeal Procedure
Internal Revenue Service

At any stage of procedure:
Agreement and payment may be arranged.

Requests for issuance of a notice of deficiency to allow petition to the Tax Court may be made.

The tax may be paid and a refund claim filed.

Examination of income tax return
District Director's Office

Preliminary notice
30-Day Letter

Protest
(when required)

Appeals Division

If no response or the time of issuing a Statutory Notice becomes short then

Statutory notice
90-Day Letter

CHOICE OF ACTION

Pay tax and file claim for refund

No tax payment

Petition to Tax Court

Consideration of claim for refund
District Director's Office

Preliminary notice
30-Day Letter

Protest
(when required)

Appeals Division

Appeals Division
Settlement opportunities if T/P has not yet been to Appeals

No agreement

Regional Counsel
Preparation for Trial

Statutory notice
Claim Disallowance

Tax Court
No Appeal Permitted in Cases Handled Under Small Tax Case Procedure

CHOICE OF ACTION

District Court

Court Of Appeals

Court Of Claims

U.S. Supreme Court

To the Courts 12

Internal Revenue's flow chart, "Income Tax Appeal Procedure," is a necessary adjunct to this chapter. There are many options if a taxpayer decides to appeal his proposed assessment through the courts.

Each option presents further choices, usually requiring either legal or practical experience to make the proper decision. Internal Revenue makes it seem easy; in Publication 556, it says, "If you and the Service still disagree after your conference, or if you skipped our appeals system, you may take your case to the United States Tax Court, the United States Court of Claims, or your United States District Court." This is an oversimplification. Even if a taxpayer is considering representing himself when he appeals to Tax Court, he should consult with a tax attorney beforehand. The issues should be evaluated and the decision to appeal further carefully reconsidered. If the appeal effort is to be continued, the choice of court is almost as important as the legal argument to be made there. (Lawyers call this "forum shopping.")

First of all, a taxpayer need not appeal within the IRS, using the appellate conference method. He can take his case directly to the United States Tax Court, still without paying the increased taxes. Sometimes, petitioning the Tax Court is simpler than writing an effective protest letter to the IRS. But, obviously, going to court will also involve

hiring counsel, preparing for trial, and working up briefs on the issues, all of which are time consuming.

Time, however, may be the deciding factor. To obtain a conference with IRS' regional appeals office, a taxpayer must file his protest letter within 30 days. To petition the Tax Court, a taxpayer ordinarily has 30 days, plus the time it takes Internal Revenue to get out the "90-day letter" (Statutory Notice of Deficiency), plus the 90 days allowed by the statutory notice. (The IRS could accelerate this schedule when the statute of limitations is about to run out, but a taxpayer always gets at least 90 days.)

A taxpayer need not use the U.S. Tax Court either. He may pay his deficiency when assessed, then file a claim for a refund (which must be done within two years). This route ultimately leads either to a federal District Court or the Court of Claims, at the taxpayer's choice. These courts serve the same purpose, but involve different internal procedures, appeal rights and other considerations. If the case is one which a jury of the taxpayer's peers will understand better than a judge selected at random (farm expenses, for example), the local federal District Court might be an appropriate choice. On the other hand, complicated depreciation or other business and investment tax questions generally tend to get a better hearing in the Court of

Claims, particularly when there is a challenge to an IRS ruling or regulation. Questions of statutory interpretation (one section says "no" and another section "yes") get more thoughtful consideration in U.S. Tax Court. The Tax Court has a reputation of being pro-IRS, but this reputation is undeserved. It is probably a reflection of the tendency of many taxpayers to take weak tax cases to the Tax Court.

A Warning

A word of warning: before you go any further (at the 90-day letter stage) understand that going to court may expose you to a countersuit by Internal Revenue's or the Justice Department's tax lawyers. Such a countersuit can be on distinctly different issues than the ones in your original suit, though it must pertain to the same year or years of taxes placed before the court.

In Tax Court you are especially vulnerable, since the U.S. Tax Court can determine any deficiency it wants. Once you file a Tax Court petition the limitation statute on the tax assessment involved is supended, or "tolled," and held open during the entire court process including appeals. Any new issues resolved against a taxpayer in the Tax Court can result in a greater deficiency than he took there in the first place. In one notable case, a taxpayer started with a $16,000 deficiency and ended with one in excess of $1 million.

In a tax refund suit in a district court or in the Court of Claims, there is also undesirable exposure to losing on another issue. Properly handled, it would generally be unlikely that you would lose more than you are suing for in these courts. A countersuit in these courts can be avoided by taking the statute of limitations into consideration when planning the timing of your case.

Your tax counsel should be informed if you have any reason to suspect that a countersuit

is possible. This might involve problems with the same or other years still open "under the statute," which the examining agent overlooked, didn't mention, or even resolved in your favor orally. If you go to Tax Court, you get no benefit whatsoever from the agent's oversight or benevolence on these problem issues; they just might whet the appetite of a trial attorney in Washington.

However, a refund suit or a case taken to Tax Court may present an opportunity to win more than the IRS placed in contention at the conclusion of the audit process or in the 90-day letter. A taxpayer who had inadvertently overpaid, or not previously contested an issue to avoid a hassle, might now bring these issues before the court.

Tax Court

The United States Tax Court is the primary level of appeal outside the Internal Revenue Service. As its name implies, this court deals strictly with tax (income, state, gift, and excess profits) matters. The court itself is located in Washington, D.C., but it holds its sessions nationwide, sitting regularly in 100 different cities, as the need arises.

Cases are accepted by the Tax Court only when an IRS assessment has not yet been fully paid, and after the IRS has issued its 90-day letter, the "notice of deficiency." You can go to Tax Court as long as there is some deficiency at the time the 90-day letter is issued, even if the deficiency is paid by the time you actually file your petition to Tax Court. (The interest clock can be stopped fully or partially by paying all or part of the amount claimed by the IRS. You cannot take your case to a district court or the Court of Claims unless the whole tax is paid beforehand, though.)

"Small tax cases" are handled under a separate set of rules by the Tax Court. A "small tax case" is one where the amount in dispute is less than $5,000 for any one taxable

FORM 2

PETITION (Small Tax Case)
(Available—Ask for Form 2)

(See Rules 170 through 179)

UNITED STATES TAX COURT

....
Petitioner(s)
v.
COMMISSIONER OF INTERNAL REVENUE,
Respondent

Docket No.

PETITION

1. Petitioner(s) request(s) the Court to redetermine the tax deficiency(ies) for the year(s) ...., as set forth in the notice of deficiency dated ....,

A COPY OF WHICH IS ATTACHED. The notice was issued by the Office of the Internal Revenue Service at ....
(City and State)

2. Petitioner(s) taxpayer identification (e.g. social security) number(s) is(are) ......
....

3. Petitioner(s) make(s) the following claims as to his tax liability:

Year	Amount of Deficiency Disputed	Addition to Tax (Penalty), if any, Disputed	Amount of Overpayment Claimed
....	....	....	....
....	....	....	....

4. Set forth those adjustments, i.e. changes, in the notice of deficiency with which you disagree and why you disagree.

....
....
....
....
....

Petitioner(s) request(s) that the proceedings in this case be conducted as a "small tax case" under section 7463 of the Internal Revenue Code of 1954, as amended, and Rule 172 of the Rules of Practice and Procedure of the United States Tax Court. *(See page 8 of the enclosed booklet.) A decision in a "small tax case" is final and cannot be appealed by either party.

....
Signature of Petitioner

Present Address   Street, City, State, Zip Code   Telephone No.

....
Signature of Petitioner (Spouse)

Present Address   Street, City, State, Zip Code   Telephone No.

....
Signature and address of counsel, if retained by petitioner(s)

*If you do not want to make this request, you should place an "X" in the following box []

year. This limit was raised to $5,000 from $1,500 on June 1, 1979.

If a dispute is handled under the small tax case rules, no further appeal is allowed. The decision of the Tax Court is final and binding on both the taxpayer and the Internal Revenue Service. Moreover, prior decisions of this part of Tax Court can't be used as precedent; each case is judged by its own merits.

There are many advantages to taking a dispute with the IRS to Tax Court as a small tax case. First of all, it is likely to be less expensive. Internal Revenue cannot take the case to another court in the hopes of a decision in its favor. The taxpayer does not have to pay defending himself against prolonged IRS appeals.

A taxpayer's petition to Tax Court in a small tax case is simplicity itself. No letter is needed, just a form stating the facts and why the taxpayer disagrees wth the IRS. The filing fee is only $10. A copy of the notice of deficiency must be attached to the petition. The papers should be sent by registered mail, to get a receipt proving the petition was filed within the 90-day limit. A copy of the petition form (Form 2) can be found in this chapter.

When a petition is filed, the taxpayer should also request that the trial be held in a city of his choice. If the taxpayer, as petitioner, does not ask, the IRS gets its choice. The petitioner's requested location will be approved unless there are not enough Tax Court cases scheduled for that city to make a court session feasible.

In a small tax case trial, strict adherence to the usual rules of evidence is not required; "any evidence deemed by the Court to have probative value shall be admissible." Proceedings are quite informal, more like a traffic court than the usual federal court. Neither briefs nor oral arguments before the court are required. A stenographic record of the pro-

ceedings is made, but a transcript is not unless the presiding judge deems it is necessary.

Because of the relaxed rules, a taxpayer may represent himself before the Tax Court; this is called *pro se* by the legal trade. Normally, *pro se* is not suggested, even for small tax cases, because the IRS will be represented by expert legal talent; there is no point in giving the IRS any more advantage than it has already. One should consider the taxpayer who, a number of years ago, was arguing *pro se* before the Chief Judge of the Tax Court. "May God be my judge," he concluded, "I don't owe these taxes." The Chief Judge smiled and responded from the bench, "He's not; I am; you do."

A petitioner may be represented either by an attorney or a non-attorney admitted to practice before the Tax Court. Non-attorneys, usually tax specialists of some sort, must pass special written and oral exams before being allowed to represent petitioners before the court.

If a taxpayer chooses for one reason or another to appear for himself, he should prepare well beforehand. Informal proceedings do not mean that the trial is not a serious and potentially expensive matter. His advisor might be able to coach him on court procedures and on the likely tactics of the IRS. Better yet, his advisor might be able to convince him to hire an attorney. (Attorneys say, "A lawyer who represents himself has a fool for a client." The same applies to taxpayers in a tax case unless the law is clear and the facts are very simple.)

If a taxpayer is determined to represent himself, a day listening to a case or two at a session of Tax Court held in a nearby city will help him get the feel and tempo of a tax trial.

The most important advantage of petitioning the Tax Court is that it often makes Internal Revenue more anxious to settle. This is particularly true in cases where more than one issue permits swapping, and when the trial preparation has not yet been completed. Government trial lawyers are only human; if their work has all been done, they tend to want to see the case go to trial.

Up to the point of petition, any initiative for a compromise settlement must come from the taxpayer; Internal Revenue only asks that its assessment be paid in full. Once a petition is filed in Tax Court, IRS' appeals division will consider the contested settlement a "docketed case." Such docketed cases receive special treatment. Internal jurisdiction may lie with either the appeals division or the Chief Counsel's office, depending on how far along the case has progressed toward trial.

Regardless of whether "appeals" or the Chief Counsel controls the case, extra effort will be made to settle before trial. Internal Revenue may even take the initiative, contacting the taxpayer or his representative to invite them in to try to reach a compromise. If not, and you want to talk issue settlement or to horse trade, don't wait until the day of the trial; settlements on the courthouse steps are just a myth.

Never ignore such settlement opportunities, as much as you would like a day in court to obtain "justice." A good settlement is always preferable to the risks of litigation. And besides, in a small tax case before the Tax Court, there's no appeal. Think settlement; the odds are in the taxpayer's favor. In 1978, 73 percent of all docketed cases were closed by agreement with the taxpayer before trial; 8,671 cases were settled for an average of 33 percent of the amount asked for on the statutory notices.

The reason for this is that things don't always go IRS' way in Tax Court. In 1978 again, the Tax Court decided in Internal Revenue's favor only 54.4 percent of the time; 10.3 percent of the decisions were for the taxpayer and 35.7 percent were compromises, going both ways. Also, since small

tax cases have no precedent value, the IRS can settle a case without giving anything to other taxpayers on the same issue.

Information and petition forms may be obtained directly from the Tax Court. Write to the Office of the Clerk of the Court, U.S. Tax Court, 400 Second St., N.W., Washington, D.C. 20217. Ask for the pamphlet, "Election of Small Tax Case Procedure and Preparation of Petitions"; Form 2, "Petition (Small Tax Case)"; Form 4, "Request for Place of Trial"; and "Rules of Practice and Procedure, United States Tax Court." If you plan to be represented, you might as well request Form 3, "Entry of Appearance," for your advisor.

If time presses, just call the Clerk's office at 202-376-2754.

Trials conducted under the regular Tax Court rules, for cases involving more than $5,000, are a different matter. They are purely a lawyer's game, as most courts are. If your appeal is heard under these rules, you will definitely need legal and accounting help.

But still, an appeal to Tax Court, even if not under the small tax case rules, has its advantages. Once a case is docketed, the IRS will attempt to compromise just as it does in cases involving less money. Internal Revenue's record in regular Tax Court is even poorer than in small tax cases; only 47.9 percent were decided entirely in its favor in 1978.

Either the taxpayer or the IRS may appeal a decision of the regular Tax Court to the Court of Appeals.

The Other Courts

The appeal procedure flow chart at the beginning of this chapter illustrates the possibilities for further appeals.

If a taxpayer's appeal goes this far, an attorney admitted to practice before the court involved will be needed. If the taxpayer's previous advisor or attorney is not qualified, it will be necessary to retain one who is. The ante escalates at this stage.

Many appeals will arrive at this level as a result of filing a claim for a refund after the tax assessment has been paid. If Internal Revenue takes no action on a claim for a refund, after six months the taxpayer may file suit for the refund. The taxpayer has two years from that date or the date the IRS disallows his claim to make his appeal move. A taxpayer anxious to get to court can request a prompt IRS rejection of his claim to start two years running. However, according to the law, a taxpayer cannot file suit without a rejection for six months after the refund claim was filed. Suit may be initiated with either a federal district court or with the Court of Claims. Like the Tax Courts, the U.S. Court of Claims is head-quartered in Washington, D.C., but its trial judges sit around the country. In addition to its inclination to be more commonsensical in business and investment matters, it has a history of being more equitably inclined in tax cases. Its decisions can only be appealed to the U.S. Supreme Court.

With refund claims, Internal Revenue is not as anxious to reach a settlement as they are in pending Tax Court cases; they already have the taxpayer's money.

Cases appealed from Tax Court are brought to one of the 11 Circuit Courts of Appeals. (So are appeals from federal District Courts.) One circuit is limited to the District of Columbia; the other 10 each cover several states or territories.

Tax law on a given point may vary in each circuit, because in the past each circuit's Court of Appeals may have ruled differently in some tax matters. (In fact, the Tax Court now decides cases differently when appeals will go to circuits that decide differently.) The record of past decisions forms a body of precedent that can be used in each new tax case in that circuit. This is one reason the IRS

often settles, even though it has won cases in other circuits on the same point. It is also why the IRS "non-acquiescences" in some court decisions; it knows there is a possibility of a better decision elsewhere.

All four categories of courts (even the Tax Court) decide on a variety of legal problems; they are not limited to income tax cases or appeals, although the great majority of Tax Court cases involve income taxes.

Information on filing an appeal in a district court can be obtained by you or your attorney from the clerk of the U.S. District Court for your jurisdiction. His office should be listed under "United States Government" in the phone book for any city where the District Court sits.

Information about filing in the U.S. Court of Claims is available from the Clerk of the Court of Claims, 717 Madison Place N.W., Washington, D.C. 20005.

The Supreme Court

In theory, a tax appeal can be carried all the way to the United States Supreme Court. In practice, there is little chance of a taxpayer's appeal being heard at this level.

Decisions of the various Courts of Appeals, or the Court of Claims, may be taken to the Supreme Court only on *Certioari,* or "cert" as lawyers refer to it. But acceptance by the high court, "taking cert," is not by any means automatic; a Circuit court opinion or one by the full court of Claims ends it for the great majority of tax cases. The Supreme Court will only consider tax problems that involve an important issue of law, those cases it believes deserving of its time. What may seem impor-tant to them may not necessarily be important to tax practitioners or to taxpayers generally. Conversely, what may be important to tax-payers and practitioners may not appear important to the Supreme Court. No one can really tell whether they will or won't "take cert" in a case. It has been suggested that in the complex area of federal income taxation, the Supreme Court only takes those cases it can understand.

In short, very few cases of any sort are accepted by the Supreme Court; most are declined and the decision of the lower court stands. A taxpayer who reaches this point and who has won in the lower courts, has an almost certain victory, and he can usually get to this point quicker in the Court of Claims.

A taxpayer should hope that any problems he might have with Internal Revenue do not reach the Supreme Court. If they do, it is likely to be very expensive in terms of money, time, and just plain nuisance value.

In any appeal, the objective should be to compromise as quickly and at as low a level as possible. Costs of settlement should always be measured against the costs of appeal. The possibility of your winning on appeal, however, is a factor that should always be stressed to the IRS in your settlement negotiations. Since almost all tax cases are published for other taxpayers to see, one thing that always gets a supervisor's attention is the possibility of establishing a precedent unfavorable to the IRS with your case.

The ideal solution, of course, is never to be audited and never to end up in a position where an appeal to the courts seems necessary.

Avoiding an Audit 13

Audit avoidance is the game skill beyond tax avoidance. Both are legal, but avoiding an audit is more of an art. The rules of this advanced game are not as clear and, inevitably, a bit of luck is involved.

The key tactic in this game is "maintaining a low profile." Internal Revenue only has the resources to audit a small portion of the tax returns filed. It prefers to run audits only on the juiciest returns, those likely to yield the most additional taxes with the least IRS effort.

"High audit potential" to the IRS means that a taxpayer's return looks succulent, just right for squeezing. "Low audit potential" means a return seems not worth an audit; the effort would likely result in little or no additional taxes.

Obviously, the trick is to have your return look more like a dried prune than a ripe plum, to signal "low audit potential" to both the computer and the classifier. The hard part of this trick is that it must be done without resorting to fraud; all tax-significant transactions must be disclosed on the return.

If you can do this successfully, you will be manipulating the odds in your favor. The overall chance of a return being audited in a particular year are only about one in 45. Not too bad, really. The problem is that the odds are distorted because the figures include large numbers of lower-income wage earners, whose returns have little or no audit potential in the eyes of the IRS.

Most readers of this manual will have higher incomes, many from self-employment as professionals or business owners. The odds of an audit for such taxpayers are much higher, easily one in 10, even one in three for certain occupations. Realistically, anyone reading an audit survival manual is likely to have a juicy return.

Anything that can be done to lower these odds is a step in the right direction. Back to one in 45 would be nice; to one in 100 even better. The lowest possible limit is one in 1,750, the odds for a TCMP audit, against which there is no defense.

The Return Itself

A tax return is just paper, a few sheets of it. But it is all Internal Revenue has to work with. And it is all the taxpayer has to create the impression of "no more taxes here."

This advice may sound simplistic but, regardless, a return should be prepared neatly. Neatness counts with the IRS, just as it did way back in grammar school.

Typewritten entries are not needed, but a dark-ink pen, sharp-pointed, should be used. Care should be taken that all information entered on the return can be read easily. What you are trying to avoid is confusing the clerks at the IRS service center who key data from the return into the computer. If an "eight" is picked up as a "six," for example, the arithmetic will not check out. The return will be rejected by the computer, and will be subjected to scrutiny by a clerk charged with error correction.

Neatness doesn't count with the computer; it doesn't see coffee stains, erasures, crossed out or smeared figures. But a tax return passes through human hands, first the clerks' and then the classifiers', and when it does, a return should reek of precision. The form should look as if it were prepared by a compulsive personality, to whom error is anathema, even if you are not that kind of person.

A tax return should be internally consistent and the arithmetic should be correct. Before a return is mailed, all computations and entries should be double and triple checked. Special care should be taken to insure that figures from one schedule are correctly re-entered when they are carried over to another page.

When you pick up blank tax forms, make sure you have a good supply. Work the return out to completion first in pencil, erasing and correcting as necessary. Transpose the figures to another form and recheck for accuracy. Use a fresh form whenever necessary to maintain the facade of precision and compulsive neatness.

All required supporting schedules should be attached. If figures from a Form 4970, 2441, 3903, 3468, 1116, 4874, 5884, or whatever are listed on the 1040, make sure the proper form supports the entry. Anything less starts the questioning process.

Extra Documentation

Internal Revenue has a form for almost, but not quite, everything. Sometimes a taxpayer wishes there were another special form to explain the unexplicable on his return. It might occasionally be desirable to attach extra informal documentation to support an unusal item on a return.

For example, imagine a single taxpayer living in Maryland, earning $25,000. Further, suppose that he bought a sailboat for $30,000 cash, paying from his accumulated savings. Maryland has a five percent sales tax; five percent of $30,000 is $1,500. However, IRS' optional sales tax tables allow this individual only a $221 deduction for state sales tax.

If he were to take a deduction for sales tax of $1,500 plus, which would be real enough, the DIF process would surely kick out his return. It would end up in the hands of a classifier who must decide if an audit is warranted.

In a special situation such as this, it might be a good idea to attach a photocopy of the bill of sale, showing the $1,500 sales tax item. If it seemed reasonable, if the rest of the return contained no questionable items, the classifier might decide to accept the return as filed, without audit.

Tax experts differ on their advice about the extra documentation ploy. Some feel that extra pieces of paper only tend to attract attention. In cases similar to the above, the classifier might be prompted to opt for an audit to determine where the taxpayer obtained his ready cash.

Of course, the taxpayer could have explained on the bill of sale that his money came from the sale of property the previous year. But then, the classifier might want to see if last year's sale was properly reported and taxed.

Obviously, supporting documentation is no cure-all. A general recommendation would be to use such extra paper only rarely, after consulting with your tax advisor, and after first determining whether or not the IRS does have a supplemental form for just such cases.

Show and Tell

In your eagerness to score well in the audit avoidance game, do not omit items of income that should be reported. Discovery of a willful omission by an auditor will entitle you to years of attention by the IRS. You should avoid even a suggestion of fraud.

If you are audited, it is important to have played by the rule: "When in doubt, report it." Exactly how you reported it is another thing entirely. What you are actually doing at tax filing and audit time is playing financial "show and tell" with Internal Revenue.

The characterization of an income item on your return is all important. Suppose you went into a venture with a relative to buy and resell a piece of property, and that your share of the profits has been returned to you. Filing a partnership return for this one-shot venture will only attract needless attention. You can report your share as a separate sale or exchange of property, but this will only mean extra paper and attention too. But if you willfully omit the income from your return, you have almost certainly committed a criminal tax offense.

In such a situation, "miscellaneous income" becomes a marvelous catchall on your return. Your share of the net proceeds from such deals can be reported as ordinary income, with only a short description, "proceeds from venture, lot, coins, etc." The point is not to omit reporting an income item, but not to over-disclose it either. Understating income will needlessly put you on the defensive, when or if you are picked for an audit.

Such situations are not always clear cut. Suppose, for example, that the transaction aborted or was incomplete at filing time. Suppose further that your venture partner had sent you to a distant city as part of the deal and paid for your expenses. If the reimbursement were reported as income, and then offset with the expenses incurred, this would only raise your visibility and perhaps trigger an unnecessary audit. Perhaps a Schedule C should be filed for such business or investment sidelines. The judgment of a tax expert is needed in such

cases. Payment of a modest fee may be necessary, but it should be remembered that such fees are deductible, and that the wrong decision may lead to years of audit entanglement with the IRS.

Bonuses

In audit avoidance, the classifier is the important audience. He is the person at whom a taxpayer's neatness and apparent precision is aimed.

Some expert players like to throw in an extra chip to convince the classifier of their honesty. They report an item or two of incidental income, the type of items most taxpayers would conveniently forget. This extra item might be a prize, gambling winnings, a recovered bad debt, or even a wife's babysitting income.

Other experts withhold questionable deductions, to use later as chips if an audit arises. Still others, in a situation where no taxes will be due if every allowable deduction or credit is claimed, will skip some and pay some tax, just to avoid a "0" on the bottom line and an audit on a high gross income return.

Some also feel that if the tax form bears the signature of a CPA or an attorney as the preparer, it may help to avoid an audit. The theory goes that such professional help is presumed to be more conscientious, to allow their clients less leeway than lesser-qualified tax preparers. The success of this tactic probably depends on the classifier's past experience with tax lawyers and CPAs.

Using a tax preparer can also backfire against a taxpayer. The IRS has a new program aimed at aggressive and negligent preparers; it has announced that negligence penalties will be levied on preparers committing even minor errors such as failing to compute the new and complicated minimum tax. The next step, if Internal Revenue remains true to form, will be to put the unfortunate taxpayer, whose preparer has locked horns with the IRS, under scrutiny. Perhaps all returns prepared by a particular preparer or firm could be pulled and examined.

A logical counter to such IRS tactics is to have a preparer work up the figures with the taxpayer taking the return home to finalize and file himself, without a tax preparer's signature. (However, some tax preparers believe that they are required to sign any return on which they have done any work at all. Others will agree to "review" a return that is already prepared by the taxpayer, and to bill the taxpayer for tax "consulting" services.) A well-typed return, signed by a well-known firm of accountants or tax preparers, is not necessarily a plus for a taxpayer trying for a low profile.

When to File

Tax returns filed early, nearer January 1 than April 15, reportedly have a much greater chance of being audited.

The reason given is that returns trickle into the service centers, building up to a rush as the mid-April deadline nears. At the beginning of the year, the examination division is under pressure to get the yearly audit program started. With fewer returns on the district inventory file, the odds of audit for a particular return soar.

A borderline return, of medium audit potential, stands a greater chance of being ignored in the great filing rush after April 1.

To file after the deadline of April 15 greatly increases the chance of an audit. Returns of late filers are given special attention, and are considered to have a higher than normal audit potential.

Rounding Off

Whenever it is necessary to estimate expenses on a return it is a good idea not to round

off the figures. Somehow, $300 as an entry looks like a hip-shot guess; $314.25 or $287.60 seems precise even if still a guess. To a classifier, figures such as $200, $250, $350, $375, are little yellow tags proclaiming "estimate—no receipts available," and an invitation to audit.

Low Profile Occupations

Any taxpayer in a high-audit-potential occupation should try to downplay it on his 1040. Certain trades and occupations are always suspect to the IRS, mainly because in these businesses cash transactions are the rule and few records are kept. The list of such occupations is long; anyone active in a suspect field undoubtedly knows why the IRS casts a wary eye on the trade.

There is no sense in waving a red flag at an IRS classifier. The "occupations" space on the tax return should be filed with an innocuous description. There is no need to lie, only not to be too specific. The owner of a small gold trading firm could call himself an "executive," an antique dealer might be a "furniture retailer," and so on. These are less glamorous job descriptions, to be sure, but also less eye-catching to a classifier.

Repeated Audits

Sometimes a taxpayer can avoid an audit just by speaking up. If an audit was performed in either of the last two years, you have ground to object if Internal Revenue proposes to examine the same items again. If the prior audit resulted in either a "no tax change" or a "small tax change" decision, just call the IRS when you receive the examination appointment letter. This only works if there is nothing significantly different in terms of issues and deductions claimed for past and present years.

Internal Revenue will want to see a copy of both the initial notification and the audit report for the years in question. The proposed audit will be postponed while the IRS checks its records. If they concur, they will probably end the audit; the IRS is not anxious to waste its auditor power where there is little chance of an assessment.

For this reason, appointment letters and audit reports from the IRS should be filed in a safe place with your copy of the return.

One tax service even recommends attaching a copy of the audit report letter, in such cases, to the next two years' returns. This acts as "supporting documentation" as discussed a few pages back. If the return is selected by the DIF process for the same reasons as in prior years, the report will give the classifier a reason to decide no audit is warranted.

Avoiding a High Profile

Membership in a "barter group" is one way to give yourself a high tax profile. Barter, exchanging goods and services directly with no money involved, is an effective way to save money and taxes. An example might be swapping a load of firewood from your property with a dentist friend who fixes two cavities in your wife's teeth. Such transactions are supposed to be reported as income by both parties, but the IRS has little hope of policing such swaps when they are privately arranged.

Formal barter clubs are another matter entirely. These are attempts to widen the barter circle, to make a greater variety of goods and services available to their members. Membership lists and records of exchanges and "credits" are maintained; some groups have even gone to computerized records.

To be active in such a group is to ask for an audit. The records are available for IRS inspection; by summons, if necessary. If you want to engage in cashless swaps and to keep a low tax profile, it is better to limit such deals to a small circle of friends.

To be a tax protestor is to automatically achieve a high profile. The IRS considers most of the usual protest patterns to be illegal. These include blank 1040s, refusal to pay based on constitutional grounds, mail-order religions, and arguments about the validity of the U.S. dollar and its lack of gold backing. Service centers routinely forward all returns with such protests to the Criminal Investigation Division for action.

A business association with an audit-prone individual can lead to your own audit. This is especially true if this person's tax evasion efforts are a more-or-less open secret to those he deals with, or if cash kickbacks are involved. Eventually, the IRS will get around to auditing all those who show up on the evader's books.

Very few businesses are "clean" by Internal Revenue's standards. However, if you have been transacting any sort of business with someone with chronic tax troubles, it might be a good idea to review the situation with your tax advisor.

Appeals Coordinated Issues List

Tax advice might be needed in another area if audit liability is to be minimized.

For years, the IRS maintained a "prime issues list," of items on which it would not compromise. Because of unfavorable publicity, there is no more "prime issues list," at least under that name.

Now there is an "Appeals Coordinated Issues List," which the IRS says it will use to help treat taxpayers in different regions more uniformly. Basically, the IRS will not settle with a taxpayer on any item on this list. The problem is that the list is still "secret" as this is being written. Informed opinion suspects that, when finally made public, the new list will contain many of the old prime issues.

If an item on this list appears on your return, the IRS will undoubtedly challenge you. To insure that you don't trigger an audit with an "appeals coordinated prime issue," your return should be prepared or reviewed by a knowledgeable professional if you are deducting items or excluding receipts which are not listed in either an IRS publication like "Your Federal Income Tax" or by a reputable tax service.

Aggressive Deductions

Most of the advice given so far on avoiding an audit is in the low profile vein: "Keep your head down and the IRS won't call on you."

But such tactics can only be taken so far. At one point or another, a taxpayer must ask himself, "If I'm never audited, does that mean I'm paying too much in taxes?" And the answer, predictably, will be, "Yes, maybe I am."

A taxpayer engaged in a continual audit battle with Internal Revenue at least knows one thing. He is maximizing his deductions and minimizing his taxes, to the extent that the IRS will let him. Of course, he is paying a price in aggravation and for accounting and legal help.

Taxpayer's temperaments vary. A level of conflict that a combative individual might thrive on would leave another worried and sleepless.

Each taxpayer must decide how aggressive a game he is willing to play. A good place to start is in consultation with a tax advisor; it helps to have a professional whose philosophy you can live with. Their ideas on playing the game vary. Many will advocate total compliance, "lying down" and taking what the IRS dishes out. Others believe in full-scale battle, making Internal Revenue sweat for every penny.

The best tactics are probably somewhere in between. Maintain as low a profile as possible for as long as you can, and yet take as many deductions as it is possible to substantiate. But do not omit income items that are not questionable, nor claim deductions not incurred.

This is playing the audit lottery game at the highest level, where it is both an art and a skill. It is still a game of chance, because the IRS can't audit everyone. By taking every possible deduction and claiming every credit without resorting to fraud, you are only exercising your rights as a taxpayer.

If you are not audited, you have successfully minimized your taxes. If your return is examined, it is likely that the IRS will claim an assessment. You may be able to counter with some unclaimed deductions (charge account interest, income averaging, investment credit, or child care perhaps). But at some level, balancing off the costs of paying the assessment and the cost of appealing, you will come to an agreement. Even then, there is a good chance that you will end up paying less than you would have if you were a totally submissive taxpayer.

What it all boils down to is that you can play the game anyway you like. Internal Revenue's reactions are predictable, if they ever get around to noticing you. And, of course, the more you know about the rules, the more comfortable and flexible you will be in this compulsory annual game.

Closing Thoughts 14

Taxes are the great curse of civilization. They have been with us ever since man ceased to be a nomad, settled down on a piece of land, and became accessible to the tax collector.

Few people would really object to paying limited taxes for necessary projects. The problem is that our society has grown so complex that we no longer can agree on what is necessary.

Government by pressure groups has become the norm. The louder the demands, the more a group becomes a threat to the peace and safety of the majority, the more money is spent on their wishes.

Fortunately, in the last few years, taxpayers have formed their own pressure groups. In the long run, there is hope for an easing of the burden on the producers, the middle class, and perhaps for a reduction in the size of government.

Many authorities estimate that government now takes 45 to 55 percent of an individual's income. State and local governments take their shares, but the federal government grabs the most. The introduction of tax withholding and "short forms" have made it easier for politicians to collect heavy taxes; only a minority (mainly middle-class entrepreneurs) regularly face the irritating chore of completing complicated forms and actually writing a check for their taxes.

The national government has an advantage in the battle for the national wealth; what it can't take directly through taxes it can take through the great invisible tax, inflation. If the federal government's revenues do not equal what it wants to spend, it spends anyway. It just creates the money to pay its deficit bills.

As the money supply increases because of the new money pumped into the economy, everyone suffers. A 10 percent inflation rate is a 10 percent tax, a tax on everything from a hamburger to the contents of a savings account. The federal government even taxes inflation; progressive tax rates hit those taxpayers whose incomes rise into higher tax brackets. Not only the national wealth erodes, but the national spirit as well. Patriotism no longer counts; it becomes foolish in the face of government greediness.

With the federal government taking more than a reasonable share and wasting most of it, it behooves a prudent taxpayer to hold onto as much as he can. If, in the long run, there is hope, in the short run it is every taxpayer for himself.

Of course, as has been stressed throughout this manual, help is available. Past a certain level of income and complication, a tax advisor becomes a necessity. Even with competent tax advice, though, it remains a taxpayer's money at risk. A prudent man should not totally abdicate his duty to minimize the tax bite.

But to be effective, even with an advisor, requires at least a rudimentary tax education. Fortunately, there are now some readable books for the non-technician. Reading the following should give a taxpayer enough basic tax knowledge so that he can communicate effectively with his advisor.

As a first book, *Everything You Always Wanted to Know About Taxes but Didn't Know How to Ask* by Michael Savage (Dial Press, $8.95), is recommended. The title is trite, but the book covers about the same ground as an introductory tax course for law students.

If you weren't already reading it, *The Taxpayer's Audit Survival Manual* would be the ideal second book. Instead, read the first book and then reread this one.

The New Taxpayers' Counterattack by Vernon Jacobs (Alexandria House Books, $14.95) is an introduction to many facets of tax planning, cutting your taxes legally by planning ahead.

Tax Shelters: A Complete Guide by Robert and Carol Tannenhouser (Harmony Books, $10.95; Signet Books paperback, $2.50) is a good layman's book on a specialist's topic. Tax shelters are another area where you have to know about it before you can do it.

To keep up-to-date after acquiring the basics, regular reading of a newsletter on taxes is suggested. Most tax letters, however, are written for tax professionals rather than for taxpayers. An exception is *Tax Angles* (901 N. Washington Street, Alexandria, VA 22314, $44 a year) which describes itself as a "monthly letter of tax-saving ideas, strategies, and techniques."

If offered in your area, a night school extension course on income taxes might also be a good way to further your tax education, especially if you want to prepare your own tax returns.

Priorities

And let us now close on this thought. You can't afford not to do something to minimize your taxes.

As an example, find the figure representing your last year's total federal income tax. Estimate your remaining working years and multiply by the tax for last year. This will give you a very rough estimate of your total federal income taxes yet to be paid, unadjusted for anything. Now take 10 percent or 20 percent of the big number, and ask yourself, "Is it worth the effort to keep this much more for myself?"

If you decide it is, then here are our recommendations:

1. Learn some more about taxes; keep up-to-date on tax law changes.
2. Find yourself a competent, compatible tax advisor, and work at cutting the fat out of your tax bill.
3. Spread the word: improve your relatives' and friends' attitudes and the quality of their tax information.
4. Only when you've done this should you join a tax reform group and work politically at cutting everyone's taxes.

Now that you've finished this manual, you know more about audits and the audit system than 97 percent of the population. Nevertheless, good luck at audit time!

List of Unallowable Items

Appendix 1

Editor's note: The explanations in this list of "unallowable items" are not intended to explain to a taxpayer why an item is unallowable. This list was taken from a document intended for internal use by the IRS; the explanations merely list the items that will cause a tax return to be selected out. When the appropriate code is keyed into the computer at an IRS service center, the computer generates the form letter that matches a particular unallowable item.

Please note also that Internal Revenue's list of unallowable items changes from time to time, as the tax laws are modified.

List of Unallowable Items

Code	Explanation
10	**Disability Income Exclusion**
	Taxpayer is claiming Disability Income Exclusion and is 65 or older and no indication that taxpayer lived apart from spouse for entire tax year.
14	**Gambling Winnings**
	If a Form W-2G is attached but the taxpayer failed to enter all the Gambling Winnings on the return and it is not reflected in AGI.

Code	Explanation
32	**Auto Expenses for Medical Care**
	If there is an amount in the Medical and Dental Expenses for "AUTO Mileage for Medical Use" in excess of seven (7) cents per mile, e.g. when (10) cents per mile was used. Does not apply if ACTUAL COST is used.
33	**Personal Expenses for Medical Care**
	Personal or Living Expenses (except transportation to obtain medical care) incidental to medical treatment, such as meals and lodging, health club dues, diet foods, funeral expenses, and maternity clothes.
34	**Federal Taxes**
	Income, Social Security (FICA) and Excise Taxes on autos, tires, telephone and air transportation, custom and import duties.
35	**Utility Taxes**
	Sewer, water, phone, garbage, gas, electric, etc.

Code	Explanation

36 State and Local Taxes

Hotel, meal, air fare, inheritance, stamp, poll, mortgage transfer taxes, etc. (Sales tax on autos is allowable.)

37 Auto License and Tags

Personal auto registration, tag and license taxes or fees except for residents of California, Colorado, Indiana, Iowa, Maine, Massachusetts, Mississippi, Nevada, Oklahoma, Washington, Wyoming, and New Hampshire.

38 Support for Child or Other Individual

If there is an amount for support of an individual (not to be confused with Child Care) claimed in miscellaneous deductions.

39 Personal Legal Expenses

Expense for wills, trusts, adoption, divorce and other items not connected with the production of income. Do not include "Attorney Fees" and "Legal Fees."

40 Educational Expenses

Educational and related expenses for other than taxpayer or spouse (tuition, books, transportation, lodging, etc., for children or other individuals).

41 Auto Expenses Related to Contributions

Auto mileage for contributions in rendering services to charitable organizations, excess of seven (7) cents per mile, e.g., ten (10)

cents per mile. Does not apply if ACTUAL COST is used.

42 Contributions

Contributions to individual or non-qualifying organizations, such as foreign charities (except Canadian Charities), lobbying organizations, etc. Also the monetary value of the taxpayer's time and labor.

Note: Contributions to political parties and/or candidates may only be claimed as a tax credit, limited to $50 per taxpayer.

43 Auto Expenses for Trade or Business

If there is an amount claimed for trade or business transportation in excess of:
1. Eighteen and one-half (18.5) cents per mile for the FIRST 15,000 miles and
2. Ten (10) cents per mile for the miles OVER 15,000 miles.

44 Casualty or Theft Loss

Losses which in themselves are unallowable, such as termite losses, lost but not stolen items, etc. The unallowable amount must be $100 or more.

45 Sale of Personal Residence

Expenses for sale or purchase of personal residence (closing expenses, settlement fees, legal fees, realtor commission, etc.) unless these items are specifically claimed as part of Moving Expense.

Code	Explanation

46   Personal Insurance

Life, auto, home, liability, etc., not claimed as Employees Business Expense.

48   Personal Living Expenses

Other personal family living expenses such as commuting to and from work, household expenses, maintenance of personal residence or auto, etc. Commuting to second job from first job is allowable.

50   Duplicate Deduction for Child Care

Credit for Child Care claimed on Line 40, Form 1040 and on Schedule A as an itemized deduction.

66   Fractional Exemption

If a taxpayer is claiming a fractional exemption for reasons other than birth, death, or community property state.

69   Foreign Tax Credit

The credit is claimed as a credit on Page 2 and as a deduction on Schedule A. Enter the amount from Schedule A as the unallowable amount.

70   Surviving Spouse

If children are claimed and the date of death listed is more than 2 years prior to the year of the return (only if dependent child claimed). This code will be identified by Unpostables.

80   Loss on Personal Residence

If Schedule D information or entries on Schedule A or other schedules report a loss on the sale of a personal asset not related to business (such as furniture, jewelry, automobile, personal residence, including loss on sale of residence on Schedule D, BUT NOT SALE OF STOCKS), do not attempt to make a change or adjustment regarding the loss.

81   Protest

If a Protest Letter, attachment, or any similar indication is present, determine whether any credit deduction tax or other amount has been omitted, adjusted, changed, deducted, revised, etc., as a Protest.

82   Duplicate Deduction

If any duplicate deductions, such as interest or taxes is claimed in two different places on the return; e.g., Page 1 or 2 of Form 1040 and Schedule A; enter Unallowable Code 82 and the amount from the duplicated deduction. This applies only when the same amount is deducted TWICE. However, it is possible and allowable for the taxpayer to deduct taxes for different purposes on various schedules.

83   Vow of Poverty

Wages on Form W-2 are from non-religious sources.

85   Civil Service Retirement System

Federal, State or Local Municipality employee deducted or excluded Civil Service Retirement System contributions. Enter a-

Code	Explanation	Code	Explanation
	mount deducted or excluded, if determinable. Ascertain occupation via Form W-2 and/or occupation box.	99	**Unspecified Unallowable**
98	**Multiple (More Than Three Unallowables)**		Anything not specifically covered that appears to be unallowable by law and not MERELY QUESTIONABLE. Also any unallowable that would require the use of a code in the 30 or 40 series and a Schedule A is not attached or is found anywhere else on the return besides Schedule A.
	If more than three unallowable codes are identified, enter Unallowable. Code 98 without an amount instead of the third code.		

Internal Revenue Manual
Sample Workpapers
Appendix 2

Sample set of workpapers provided as an example in Internal Revenue Manual 4233.

Tax Audit Guidelines, Individuals, Partnerships,   **page 4233-25**
Estates and Trusts, and Corporations   (9-27-76)

RICHARD ABLE
500 Clay Street
Santa Fe, New Mexico

Year — 1960

Pete Smith
Internal Revenue Agent

page 4233-26   Tax Audit Guidelines, Individuals, Partnerships,
(9-27-76)   Estates and Trusts, and Corporations

Richard Able   **Year 1960**

INDEX TO WORKPAPERS

	Work Sheet	Page
Preliminary analysis	A	
Discussions	B	
Bank deposit analysis	C	
Other returns	D	
Analyses and test checks	E	
Interest income	E-1	
Rental income and expense	E-2	
Capital gains	E-3	
Contributions	E-4	
Casualty loss	E-5	
Interest expense	E-6	
Taxes	E-7	
Net worth (Illustrative Only)	E-8	
Analysis of travel and entertainment expenses (Illustrative Only)	E-9	
Foreign tax credit or deduction	F	

Tax Audit Guidelines, Individuals, Partnerships, Estates and Trusts, and Corporations

page 4233-27
(9-27-76)

Worksheet A

Richard Able

Year 1960

Preliminary Analysis
   9/7/61

1. Contributions to unusual organizations.

2. Casualty loss—No information given.

3. Capital gains—No details given.

4. No interest or dividends reported.

5. Prior examination report extended life on rental property.

Examination Findings

1. Adjustment recommended in report.

2. Loss allowed—See Worksheet E-5.

3. No adjustment, details procured—See Worksheet E-3.

4. Adjustment recommended in report. Also, see Worksheet E-1.

5. Adjustment recommended in report.

Worksheet B

Richard Able

Year 1960

Discussions
9/8/61

Taxpayer is married. He resides with his spouse and three children in a brick veneer ranch home in an average residential area. The home, from the portion observed, is modestly furnished. Taxpayer's children are ages 16, 14 and 13. They attend a public high school.

Taxpayer is 45 years of age. He has worked for his present employer for 25 years. His present earnings are $14,000, and his salary has never exceeded this amount. He received no expense reimbursements or allowances. Taxpayer formerly was an inactive partner in the XYZ Partnership. This company incurred substantial losses, and the taxpayer went through bankruptcy proceedings in 1954.

Taxpayer's spouse owns a rental property. It is presently rented for $100 per month. Taxpayer's spouse also has common stock holdings in the ABC Corporation. The rental property and stock were inherited by the spouse from her mother.

The taxpayer and his spouse maintain separate checking accounts, and the spouse also has a savings account. They have one automobile, a Cadillac.

The taxpayer indicated that they had no other assets, and that they do not keep any substantial amounts of cash on hand. He also stated that there were no dispositions of assets, other than those reported and that he had not received any tax-exempt or nontaxable income.

Tax Audit Guidelines, Individuals, Partnerships,
Estates and Trusts, and Corporations

page 4233-29
(9-27-76)

Worksheet C

Richard Able

Year 1960

Bank Deposit Analysis

	City Bank (Husband)	County Bank (Wife)	
1960			
Jan.	1,000		Salary
		500	Transfer from City Bank
Feb.	1,000		Salary
Mar.	1,000		Salary
April	1,000		Salary
May	1,000		Salary
June	1,000		Salary
		14,000	Down payment on 41 acres
July	1,000		Salary
Aug.		24,000	Balance on 41 acres
	1,000		Salary
Sept.	1,000		Salary
Oct.	1,000		Salary
	500		Transfer from County Bank
Nov.	1,000		Salary
Dec.	1,000		Salary

Note—Collections from rental property are received in cash by spouse and deposited.

Taxpayer and spouse do not maintain any brokerage accounts.

Savings' account of spouse was not analyzed. Only transactions reflected therein relate to deposit of stock proceeds and interest credits.

Worksheet D

Richard Able

Year 1960

Other Returns

A perusal of the 1958 and 1959 returns did not reveal any items worthy of examination. Interest was correctly reflected. Other items were apparently substantially similar to 1960.

Worksheet E

Richard Able   Year 1960

Analyses and Test Checks

                                              Worksheet

                           Analyses

1. Interest income   E-1
2. Rental income and expense   E-2
3. Capital gains   E-3
4. Contributions   E-4
5. Casualty loss   E-5

                          Test Checks

1. Interest expense   E-6
2. Taxes   E-7

                        Other Procedures

1. Net worth (Illustrative Only)   E-8
2. Analysis of travel and entertainment   E-9
   expenses
      (Illustrative Only)

Worksheet E-1

Richard Able   Year 1960

Interest Income
County Bank – Spouse's savings account

6/30/60	Interest credit to a/c	50
12/31/60	Interest credit to a/c	75
	Total received	125
	Amount reported	-0-
	Adjustment	125

Taxpayer indicated that this income was inadvertently omitted from the return.

The ABC Corporation did not pay any dividends in 1960.

Tax Audit Guidelines, Individuals, Partnerships, Estates and Trusts, and Corporations

Worksheet E-2

Richard Able

Year 1960

Rental Income and Expense

House - 1910 Washington Street	Return	Corrected	Adjustment
(a) Total rents	1100	1100	
Depreciation	600	300	300
(b) Repairs	150	150	
(c) Other - Taxes	350	350	—
Total expenses	1100	800	300
Net income from rents	-0-	300	300

(a) Property is rented at $100 per month. Prior tenant terminated tenancy, and property was vacant for one month.

(b) Repairs—Receipted invoices were submitted to substantiate full amount of expense. Description on invoices revealed all expenditures to be repairs.

(c) Taxes—Receipted tax bill was submitted. No special assessments were included in payment. Depreciation—Prior examination report extended useful life from 10 years to 20 years. The corrected life has been used in making the adjustment herein.

Valuation in gross estate of spouse's mother	8,000
Less: Land	2,000
Basis of buildings	6,000
Depreciation allowable @ 5%	300
Depreciation claimed @ 10%	600
Adjustment	300
Reserve for depreciation @ 12/31/59	*600
Depreciation allowed for 1960	300
Reserve for depreciation @ 12/31/60	900

*Per prior examination report

Worksheet E-3

Richard Able   Year 1960

Capital Gains

Property	Date Acquired	Date Sold	Gross Sales Price	Basis	Expense of Sale	Gain
Land	1957	6/6/60	40,000	37,000	2,000	1,000
Stock	1957	11/10/60	15,000	14,500	300	200
			55,000	51,500	2,300	1,200

The sales price and expenses of sale on the land and stock were compared with closing and brokerage statements that the taxpayer submitted.

The basis of the property was verified with the value included in the gross estate, as the taxpayer's spouse inherited this property from her mother.

Worksheet E-4

Richard Able   Year 1960

Contributions

	Return	Allowed	Disallowed
Community Chest	200	200	
Y.M.C.A.	100	100	
Church	300	300	
(a) Good Fellows League	375		375
(a) Hoofers Club	350	___	350
	1325	600	725

The taxpayer submitted cancelled checks on all claimed contributions, and the endorsements thereon were scrutinized.

(a) These contributions were not made to recognized charitable organizations.

Worksheet E-5

Richard Able   Year 1960

Casualty Loss

The taxpayer was involved in an automobile accident with his car. He did not carry collision insurance, and there was no recourse or recovery from the other party involved in the accident. The loss deduction claimed represents the actual cost of the repairs resulting from the collision. The difference in fair market values of the auto before and after the casualty was greater than the cost of the repairs.

Tax Audit Guidelines, Individuals, Partnerships,
Estates and Trusts, and Corporations

Worksheet E-6

Richard Able

Year 1960

Interest Expense

The taxpayer claimed deductions for·the interest element included in carrying charges on several conditional sale contracts. The taxpayer's computations were checked, and were found to be reasonably correct.

Worksheet E-7

Richard Able

Year 1960

Taxes

The taxpayer claimed deductions for real estate taxes, sales taxes and state license and gasoline taxes. The real estate tax deduction was compared with the receipted property tax bill. The sales and gasoline taxes deducted are reasonable considering the taxpayer's standard of living and mileage driven.

Worksheet E-8

Richard Able   Year 1960

<u>*Net Worth*</u> (Illustrative Only)
12/31/60

Year	Income	Tax & Living Expenses	Net Accretion	Inheritance	
1955	8,000	8,000	--		
1956	8,000	8,000	--		
1957	11,000	11,000	--	70,000	70,000
1958	26,000	11,000	15,000		15,000
1959	15,000	15,000	--		
1960	<u>16,000</u>	<u>14,000</u>	<u>2,000</u>	<u> </u>	<u>2,000</u>
	<u>84,000</u>	<u>67,000</u>	<u>17,000</u>	<u>70,000</u>	<u>87,000</u>

Balance of property after 1954 bankruptcy

   Residence   <u>8,000</u>

        Total Funds reported available   <u>95,000</u>

Total Assets Now Owned:

Cadillac	4,000
Savings account	21,000
Home (Exchange basis)	8,000
Bank account—Husband	1,000
Bank account—Wife	36,000
ABC stock	10,500
Rental property (Inheritance basis)	8,000
Furnishings	<u>6,500</u>
	<u>95,000</u>

Tax Audit Guidelines, Individuals, Partnerships,
Estates and Trusts, and Corporations

Worksheet E-9

Richard Able

Year 1960

Analysis of Travel and Entertainment Expenses (Illustrative Only)

1	2	3		4		5	6	7
		Supported by Voucher		No Voucher				
Category of Expense	Claimed on Return	Paid by Check	Paid by Cash	Paid by Check	Paid by Cash	Allowed	Disallowed	Explanation
Travel	$500			$500			$500	Wife's trip to New York

Column (1) – Follow schedule attached to return or Form 2106.
     (2) – Self explanatory.
     (3) – Show items examined in each category.
     (4) – Same as (3).
     (5) – Show items in (3) and (4) which were determined to be properly allowable.
     (6) – Show items in (3) and (4) which were determined to be personal or unsubstantiated.
     (7) – Explain action in (5) and (6).

Worksheet F

Richard Able

Year 1960

Foreign Tax Credit or Deduction

    The taxpayer did not claim a credit or deduction, and has no income from foreign sources.

332 *(9-27-76)*
**Individuals—Business and
Partnerships**

4233

A. B. C. PARTNERSHIP

225 Front Street

Baltimore, Maryland

Year — 1960

**Tom Jones
Internal Revenue Agent**

Note – The illustrative worksheets covering the A.B.C. Partnership are equally applicable, with
appropriate modifications, to examinations of individual returns with business or farm
schedules. The worksheets have been alphabetically designated for ready identification
with the applicable basic technique.

Internal Revenue Guidelines for Auditing Professionals Appendix 3

Guidelines for auditing Professional Persons, reproduced from Internal Revenue Manual 4231.

Chapter (12)00

Professional Persons

(12)10 *(8-30-76)*   4231
Introduction

(1) Professional persons use many different systems of recording income and expense. Many professional persons practice their professions as sole proprietors, maintain single entry systems of accounting and use the cash basis method of reporting income on their returns. In other instances where partnerships, joint ventures, and associate arrangements exist, the systems usually tend to be more formal.

(2) The income of professional persons is derived from fees for personal services. This is important for the examiner to consider in planning his/her audit, since it will be incumbent on him/her to account for fee income and related professional expenses. Usually there are no inventories nor direct costs of sales involved in earning fees. Consequently, it is seldom that reliable ratios will be available as a rule-of-thumb test in estimating receipts.

(3) Generally, the professional person will employ one or two persons such as a secretary, receptionist or nurse. If one of these persons is related to the taxpayer, the revenue agent should be alert to the possibility of collusion since an internal control may not exist. In small offices where one person is responsible for the receipt and disbursement of funds, the revenue agent should be diligent in the application of auditing tests to assure himself/herself that adequate records are maintained and that income is properly reported. The revenue agent should be alert to the numerous ways in which fee income may be omitted from the records.

(4) Many cases of unreported income have been found by revenue agents involving highly regarded professional persons, who are active in civic and religious organizations. The revenue agent is counselled in regard to audits of this type only to point out that, regardless of the identity of the taxpayer, certain auditing techniques should be used. If the tests and analyses made indicate irregularities, ingenuity and judgment should be used to bring the examination to its proper conclusion. The utilization of information in Chapter (10)00 will be beneficial in this type of case.

(5) As a general rule it can be stated that the most important feature in the audit of a professional person's return is the auditing techniques used to test for omitted income. Of course, expenses should be given appropriate attention, considering the manner of payment and whether substantial in amount.

(6) Techniques suggested herein *are not intended to be all-inclusive*, but are mentioned to point out features which are found in most professions. It would be impractical to apply all techniques in each case. The facts and circumstances in each instance should guide the revenue agent.

(12)20 *(8-30-76)*   4231
Approach

(12)21 *(8-30-76)*   4231
Precontact Analysis of the Return

(1) An audit of a professional person's return requires precontact planning as in other examinations of business type returns. When possible, computations should be made by the revenue agent to determine significant financial information about investments, capital assets purchased, and the type and size of the taxpayer's practice. Experience has shown that a source and application of funds computation prepared from the return itself will frequently reveal beneficial information.

(2) See 233 and (10)72 for detailed information that can be secured from a thorough analysis of the return before contacting the taxpayer.

(12)22 *(8-30-76)*   4231
Initial Interview

(1) Contacting the taxpayer for an appointment and arranging for records to be made available for examination is covered in Chapter 400. A well-rehearsed technique of conducting an interview that will give it a spontaneous atmosphere can be of immense value to the revenue agent. Discussion of personal items usually elicits more forthright answers during the initial interview and should therefore be as all-inclusive as possible. The initial contact, whether by phone or mail, will be of the most value if the taxpayer fully understands the exact records he/she is to have available when the revenue agent arrives for his/her appointment. It is preferable that arrangements for the examination be made with the taxpayer and that the initial interview also be held with him/her.

(2) During the initial interview, the examiner should secure the following information.

(a) Explanation of the accounting system and manner of recording fee income.

(b) What records were used to account for income?

(c) What records were used, and by whom, to prepare the return?

(d) Who handles receipts in the office, who deposits them and are they all deposited?

(e) Length of time in practice, and speciality, if any.

(f) Did the taxpayer engage in teaching, writing, or lecturing?

(g) Number of offices, interoffices or chairs (dentists, podiatrists, urologists, etc.).

(h) Investment data.

(i) Names of all bank accounts and nature (business and personal).

(j) What method is used for billing delinquent accounts? If billings are made on a specific date during the month, some response in the form of collections should be apparent in the subsequent days.

(k) Are delinquent accounts turned over to collection agencies? If so, how are ultimate collections from this agency reported?

(l) Is the taxpayer associated with universities, governmental agencies, schools, industrial concerns, life insurance companies, etc.? If so, how is such income reported?

(m) Were any services rendered without cash remuneration but in exchange for some other asset or service performed by the patient or client?

(3) Securing the above information in the initial interview will usually save many hours of examination time. Experience has shown that this is the most opportune time to secure vital information. The lack of skill in conducting this interview can be injurious to the revenue agent's case in situations where the taxpayer later refuses to cooperate. See 921 and (10)73 for other information which may be secured in the first interview with the taxpayer.

(4) The remainder of this chapter is devoted to setting forth specific information dealing with certain professions, the type of records generally found in these professions, and audit techniques which can be effectively used to test these records and to verify the reported income.

(12)30 (8-30-76)   4231
Physicians

(12)31 (8-30-76)   4231
General

(1) In examining the returns of a physician (hereinafter referred to as a doctor) it is well to

remember that, whereas he/she is highly trained in his/her profession, he/she is usually not trained or educated in the complications of accounting and taxes. Very often he/she will delegate the bookkeeping duties to an employee and depend on an accountant or attorney for tax advice. He/she is a busy person, with his/her time scheduled daily. The revenue agent, in requesting an appointment to audit his/her records, should be firm, as well as courteous.

(2) Attention is directed to the doctor who does not maintain adequate or complete records. It has also been found that doctors who have received notoriety for being involved in illegal abortions and narcotics generally maintain poor records. This should put the revenue agent on notice that other than usual auditing techniques may have to be applied. See Chapter 900.

(3) It is recognized that many doctors earn a very high income. Frequently they keep vital income records personally in order to avoid letting employees know about their business. Some have a constant turnover of clerical help to accomplish the same end. Many times fees are collected and, unknown to the employees, will be omitted from the records. The point for the revenue agent to bear in mind, regardless of the circumstances confronting him/her in each case, is how to test or audit vital parts of the records with the least amount of effort, in order to satisfy himself/herself that income has been properly reported.

(12)32 (8-30-76)   4231
Records

(12)32.1 (8-30-76)   4231
Introduction

(1) Many systems are in use by doctors to record their income and expenses, and the examiner should find in one form or another the following records:

(a) appointment book;

(b) daily log showing dates, names of patients and payments;

(c) receipt book;

(d) bank records;

(e) disbursement journal or ledger (active and inactive);

(f) recapitulation schedules or worksheets.

(12)32.2 (8-30-76)   4231
Appointment Book

The appointment book is not ordinarily used for the recording of bookkeeping entries, unless informal notations are made thereon. This record contains the listing in chronological order of appointments with patients whose names are recorded in advance, usually by the doctor's nurse or secretary. This book is the vital control of the doctor's time, and thus should indicate income activity. If a doctor states that this book has been lost or destroyed, it is very likely that the doctor does not wish to have his/her fee records probed into thoroughly. If this occurs, patient cards and other records for current and prior years should be analyzed carefully to detect errors or omissions in recording fees.

(12)32.3 (8-30-76)   4231
Daily Log

When the patient appears for his/her appointment, the visit may be recorded in a "Daily Log." A payment or charge may also be recorded after the visit. This log identifies the patient treated on the indicated date, and it is here that the charges for services are usually recorded. Receipts by mail are also usually recorded in the log.

(12)32.4 (8-30-76)   4231
Receipt Book

If a patient makes a payment in cash, a receipt is usually issued. If the receipts are serially numbered, they can easily be checked to the record containing cash payments received. If the receipts are not numbered, and this is common, it will be more difficult to establish that all receipts are recorded in income. If this situation exists, the revenue agent should make tests to satisfy himself/herself that all fees are consistently recorded as income.

(12)32.5 (8-30-76)   4231
Bank Records

(1) A vital part of the audit of a doctor's return is an analysis of the following records:
(a) check stubs and cancelled checks;
(b) bank statements—business and personal;
(c) deposit slips (or duplicates);
(d) deposit books (savings accounts).

(12)32.6 (8-30-76)   4231
Disbursement Journal or Ledger

This record may be in any form and, if disbursements are made by check, will not differ from other taxpayers' records. Expenses paid by cash should be given special attention.

(12)32.7 (8-30-76)   4231
Patients' Cards

It is customary to prepare a card for each patient. The information will vary, but essentially it will be used by the doctor for identification of the patient, and to record charges and payments (including those by mail). Sometimes the medical history will be a part of the card.

(12)32.8 (8-30-76)   4231
Recapitulation Schedules or Worksheets

(1) It is customary for doctors to prepare a schedule of fees received for each month. These schedules are then used at year's end to assist in preparing the return. The revenue agent is cautioned to make audit tests of the patient cards and daily log, rather than to rely on the monthly summary figures.

(2) Weekly or monthly totals are usually posted to a schedule to be used by the person making out the income tax return at the end of the year. If only the summaries are furnished during the audit, the revenue agent will make every effort to obtain the original records to determine that fee income has been reported correctly.

(12)33 (8-30-76)   4231
Determining Gross Income

(12)33.1 (8-30-76)   4231
Introduction

(1) When taxpayers in this category fail to keep complete records, it should alert the revenue agent that other than the usual audit procedures will apply.

(2) Many doctor's returns will show low gross receipts. This may be attributed to the taxpayer's recent start to practice, illness, or his/her aged or semi-retired condition. It also may be that the doctor simply is not capable, or does not have a profitable clientele. The correct reason should be determined as quickly as possible. However, it may be that a substantial portion of fees has been omitted from gross receipts. Whatever the reason, the revenue agent should attempt to establish the true facts before time-consuming audit procedures are undertaken.

(3) Usually medical practitioners earn more than dentists, and many surgeons and special-

MT 4231-24

(12)33.1
IR Manual

ists earn higher fees than general practitioners. The revenue agent should consult with his/her supervisor or experienced agents about some of the facts found in their experience. This will assist the agent in utilizing his/her time in these examinations, particularly in those cases where some or all of the records are not available.

(12)33.2 (8-30-76)   4231
Fees

(1) Every doctor has a scale of fees. If possible, this should be determined during the initial interview with him/her. This information permits efficient tests for receipts, charges, and fee income reported. Fees may be received from regular or referred patients, drop-in or emergency patients, insurance companies, and health and accident companies.

(2) Inquiry can be made as to how payments from health insurance companies, such as Blue Cross, are recorded. If any doubts arise, the agent should utilize, if possible, the paying agencies to verify those receipts.

(3) It has been found that practitioners sometimes fail to report fees from after hours office or house calls. If the doctor's diary can be obtained for testing, any omissions can readily be determined.

(12)33.3 (8-30-76)   4231
Other Income

(1) Frequently it will be found that a doctor will teach or lecture at medical schools. Sometimes articles or books will be written, and some doctors do work as professional lecturers. Inquiry should be made into these features to ascertain if income from these activities has been reported.

(2) At times the doctor may be called in a professional capacity as an expert witness. Inquiry should be made about the procedure followed in recording this type of income.

(3) An important feature to keep in mind in the examination of doctors' returns is that they generally earn high income and therefore have a strong incentive to minimize their income taxes. Having substantial sums available, there is usually a strong desire to invest in securities, bonds, rental properties, oil properties, and real estate. This, in turn, creates a responsibility for the revenue agent not only to audit the professional records in an efficient manner, but also to investigate investment features in these returns.

(4) Doctors who enjoy a profitable practice,

yet report little or no investment income, should be subject to close scrutiny by the revenue agent.

(5) Occasionally a doctor has income producing arrangements with other doctors or professional people. Some of these have been kickback arrangements with druggists on prescriptions, with opticians on prescriptions for glasses and frames, or with specialists on referrals. The examiner should be alert to indications that any of the above practices may exist. If the examiner has reason to doubt that these discounts or kickbacks have been properly recorded, inquiry should be made of the druggist, hospital, or specialist involved.

(12)34 (8-30-76)   4231
Verification of Income

(1) The verification of a doctor's income is a technique which calls for skill and judgment. The numerous cash transactions and the widespread absence of adequate accounting controls give rise to a possibility that a substantial portion of the income might be diverted to personal living expenses, investments or to hidden bank accounts without first being included in income. The verification of what is included in the records is a comparatively simple procedure. *It is the uncovering of what might not be in the records that tests the ingenuity and experience of the revenue agent.*

(2) In order to test the records the revenue agent should assemble the appointment book, patient cards, daily log, and deposit slips, if available, for a selected period. Some of the techniques would be:

(a) Test the footings in the daily log to the monthly recapitulation schedule, and then to the annual total gross receipts as reported on the return. Check receipts from Daily Log to deposit slips. Compare patient card financial records with Daily Log.

(b) In conjunction with the above records, effective results can also be obtained if the examiner will secure the names of several patients who have been treated for 1 to 2 years prior to the year under examination. The examiner should then secure the open and closed cards and compare them as to their completeness and for accuracy of the recording of the fees received for the entire period.

(c) Select patients' names by alphabet and taking those in one letter, test to the above records and the active and inactive patient cards.

(d) Analyze or reconcile the total deposits to gross funds available to the taxpayer. See Chapter 900 for techniques.

(12)33.1
IR Manual   MT 4231-24

(e) If some of the records are not available or all receipts are not deposited, the examiner may wish to ascertain if there has been a substantial increase in net worth in the years under review. See 930 for techniques. Frequently an informed net worth computation will indicate an unexplained source of funds. If this occurs, the examiner should bring this to the attention of his/her supervisor since fraud may be involved.

(f) If the doctor permits the agent to review the record of individual patient's medical history, similar cross checks can be made to verify that either charges or collections are recorded when services are rendered. The doctor may neglect to record appointments for patients requiring treatment at regular intervals over a long period of time and instead rely on his/her memory.

(g) In the event some records are not available, the taxpayer is uncooperative, or the examiner wishes to test the accuracy of some of the records examined, the following sources may be of assistance.

.1 *Local medical society records*—A file is maintained of all member physicians listing the hospital where each physician is associated.

2 *Hospitals*—Each hospital maintains a record of all admissions authorized by each physician. Another file is kept for all surgery performed or assisted by each physician.

3 *Public birth and death records*—These records usually indicate the name of the attending physician.

4 *Insurance company records*—(Life insurance, health and accident, hospitalization.)

5 *Pharmacies*—Druggists are required by law to keep a record of all prescriptions filled. Occasionally they also maintain a cross-index file by physician's name.

6 *Local telephone answering service.*

(12)35 *(8-30-76)*   4231
Expenses

(12)35.1 *(8-30-76)*   4231
Introduction

(1) A doctor is entitled to deduct from gross income, as ordinary and necessary business expenses, all amounts actually expended in carrying on his/her profession. Since most doctors are on the cash basis of accounting, the expenses must be paid to be deductible. Exceptions to this are depreciation, prepaid rent and insurance and other items of this type which should be deducted ratably as they expire.

(2) In the event the doctor has an office in his/her home, it will be necessary to apportion the personal and business expenses. The examiner must be alert to personal expenses claimed under the guise of business deductions.

(3) Although no specific comparison can be made between a physician's gross income and the amount of drugs and supplies he/she purchases, large expenditures for drugs and supplies would normally indicate either a large volume of business or that he/she is a combination physician-pharmacist who administers and sells preventive vaccines and drugs. However, a revenue agent should be aware that physicians do receive many free samples of drugs and supplies. Also, it is not unheard of for a medical supply house to stock personal items, such as, cameras, luggage or sports equipment. If these personal items are included in the drug expense, they should be disallowed.

(12)35.2 *(8-30-76)*   4231
Salaries and Wages

In some cases, a doctor will employ other doctors as assistants. Also, there may be a participation or bonus arrangement with them. In this event, the disbursement should be verified with the cash records. These persons are usually paid as independent contractors, not subject to withholding tax. The examiner should satisfy himself/herself that the amount received by the assistant was reported correctly. Referral fees or fee splitting payments are deductible when they are cutomary in the profession and in the community and are not prohibited by law.

(12)35.3 *(8-30-76)*   4231
Domestic Labor

The examiner should check the payroll records to determine the number of employees involved and inquire as to the duties of each, for the purpose of eliminating domestic help. Amounts paid to persons engaged in housework are not deductible. In the event the doctor maintains an office in his/her home, a proper apportionment of expenses must be made. Wages paid a chauffeur are rarely deductible.

(12)35.4 *(8-30-76)*   4231
Taxes

If the doctor owns any property, other than his/her home, and claims real estate taxes, the tax bills should be examined to eliminate any personal taxes from the business schedule.

MT 4231-24   **(12)35.4**

(12)35.5 *(8-30-76)*   4231
Bad Debts

As has been stated, most doctors report on the cash basis, which usually precludes their claiming losses from bad debts. Occasionally a fee is paid by a check which later fails to be honored by the bank. If the check was reported when received, the taxpayer would then be entitled to a deduction when the check proves bad. If the doctor reports his/her gross fees as billed, he/she would be entitled to a bad-debt deduction for fees not actually received. If delinquent accounts are turned over to a collection agency, it should be determined how recoveries are handled.

(12)35.6 *(8-30-76)*   4231
Depreciation

(1) As a general rule, depreciation will not be a significant factor in examining the return of a doctor, since capital assets are not generally a substantial factor in producing his professional income. The year and manner of the acquisition of assets should be checked, noting the financial arrangements and whether the funds used came from a properly identified source.

(2) The agent should check for duplication of expense, such as depreciation of auto. It may also be claimed in auto upkeep.

(12)35.7 *(8-30-76)*   4231
Repairs

This is not usually a significant item in a doctor's return. However, if the amount is substantial, the canceled check should be examined in conjunction with the invoice to determine the nature of the expenditure as well as to verify the actual cost.

(12)35.8 *(8-30-76)*   4231
Insurance

(1) This deduction may include such nondeductible items as life insurance and insurance on personal dwelling. Care should be taken to exclude the personal portion of insurance on autos.

(2) Another reason this expense should be carefully scrutinized is that the doctors usually have no retirement plan to provide for necessities at an advanced age and consequently are often heavily insured. They may carry life insurance, hospitalization, health and accident, business interruption insurance and also may purchase annuities. The agent should assure himself/herself that these premiums are not being paid out of unreported income nor claimed as expense.

(12)35.9 *(8-30-76)*   4231
Travel and Entertainment

(1) Under present law, any deduction for travel and entertainment must meet the long-standing statutory test of ordinary and necessary as well as the requirements of IRC 274. The examiner should pay particular attention to those doctors' returns wherein amounts are claimed for entertainment and similar expense.

(2) Many abuses have been found in this area and the examiner should be thoroughly familiar with the requirements of IRC 274 before embarking upon an audit of travel and entertainment.

(12)35.10 *(8-30-76)*   4231
Dues

Dues for membership in professional associations and civic organizations are generally deductible as ordinary and necessary business expenses. The deductibility of dues for membership in any social, athletic, or sporting club or organization, however, is subject to the provisions of IRC 274; the agent, therefore, should be familiar with these requirements prior to the audit.

(12)35.11 *(8-30-76)*   4231
Automobile

Expenses for commuting between a doctor's residence and his/her office are nondeductible regardless of the distance. The examiner will usually have the problem of apportioning auto expense as to business and personal, and the facts in each case should govern.

(12)35.12 *(8-30-76)*   4231
Education

(1) The cost of a refresher course may be allowed only to the extent that it is necessary to keep the doctor advised on new developments in his/her field. The cost of instruction in a field in which he/she has not previously engaged is not allowable. Prolonged courses would indicate new skills were being acquired.

(2) Psychoanalysts and psychiatrists frequently incur expenses for personal analyses which may be required in their profession. Such expenses usually arise near the close of their training or just prior to the start of their practice. Such expenditures are not deductible as medical or business expenses. They may possibly be deductible as educational expenses, depending upon the facts of the particular case.

136   Appendix 3: Internal Revenue Guidelines for Auditing Professionals

(12)36 *(8-30-76)*   4231
Physician and Patient—Privilege

The Federal courts have assumed the communications made by a patient to a physician, while seeking professional advice, are privileged.[1] This privilege has not been extended to financial matters, such as the amount of fees paid for professional services. The privilege has also been indirectly denied in connection with summonses issued by special agents for production of hospital records.[2] If the revenue agent is well informed on the subject of privileged matter in the doctor-patient relationship, an audit of the doctor's returns should pose no difficulty in obtaining the necessary information in regard to financial transactions of either party.

(12)40 *(8-30-76)*   4231
Dentists

(1) The accounting systems and records of dentists are very similar to that of other doctors. A dentist usually keeps an appointment and daily log book designed especially for dentists.

(2) In contrast to the examination of other doctors, the costs of supplies in a dentist's work will be higher, due to the use of gold, silver, etc.

(3) In determining the correct income, the revenue agent should verify that the sale of used precious metals has been included in gross income.

(4) Generally speaking, it will be difficult for a dentist to defend the need for extensive entertainment and travel expense and the revenue agent should be firm in his/her requests for substantiation of expense in this category.

(5) The procedures for verification of income of a doctor should be followed in the examination of a dentist's tax return.

(12)50 *(8-30-76)*   4231
Attorneys

(12)51 *(8-30-76)*   4231
Introduction

(1) It has often come to the attention of the Service, in examining the returns of attorneys, that there is a widespread practice of maintaining a minimum of accounting records. Very few attorneys keep a card index of clients; if they do, this index is rarely made available to agents in their audits. As a result of this, examiners are constantly pressed to use ingenuity in auditing available records in order to determine the accuracy of same and to evaluate the effort the taxpayer has made to correctly report his/her income. If is often necessary to resort to third-party records, such as the county court house, to determine if all fees on certain cases have been properly reported in income. In some instances it has been found that the attorney keeps a financial record of the case on the inside of the folder containing the case file. This may involve the important issue of "privileged communications" between an attorney and his/her clients, as related to an examination of an attorney's return. The revenue agent should understand this relationship in order to more successfully secure pertinent financial information when he/she is dealing with an attorney.

(2) There are certain special types of relationships in which information communicated by one person to the other is held confidential and privileged between them. In 8 Wigmore on Evidence (3d Ed.) 2285, it is stated there are four fundamental conditions that must exist:

(a) the communications must originate in a confidence that they will not be disclosed;

(b) the element of confidentialty must be essential to the full and satisfactory maintenance of the relationship between the parties;

(c) the relation must be one which in the opinion of the community ought to be sedulously fostered; and

(d) the injury that would inure to the relationship by the disclosure of the communications must be greater than the benefit thereby gained for the correct disposal of litigation.

(3) The mere relationship of attorney and client does not render confidential every communication made by the client to the attorney. If the attorney is just a conduit for handling funds, or the transaction involves a simple transfer of title to real estate, and there is no consultation for legal advice, communications made to him/her by the client are not privileged.[3]

(4) Communications made in the course of seeking business advice rather than legal advice are likewise not privileged.[4]

(5) It has been held that the privilege is inapplicable to communications made to a person

---

[1] *Mullen* v. *U.S.*, 263 F. 2d 275 (C.A., D.C.); *Totten* v. *U.S.*, 92 U.S., 105; *U.S.* v. *Kenney*, 111 F. Supp. 233 (D.C., D.C.), rev. on other grounds, 218 F. 2d 843 (C.A., D.C.)
[2] *Albert Lindley Lee Memorial Hospital*, 115 F. Supp. 643 (M.D., N.Y.) Aff'd 209 F. 2d 122 (CA-2), Cer. denied 347 U.S. 960; *Gretsky* v. *Basso*, 136 F. Supp. 640 (D.C., Mass.) 56-1 USTC 9148.

[3] *Pollock* v. *U.S.*, 202 F. 2d 281 (CA-5), 53-1 USTC 9229; *U.S.* v. *DeVasto*, 52 F. 2d 26 (C.A.-2); *McFee* v. *U.S.*, 206 F. 2d 872 (C.A.-9), 53-2 U.S.T.C. 9549; *Koerner* v. *Baird*, 59-2 USTC 9517 (S.D. California).
[4] *U.S.* v. *Vehicular Parking*, 52 F. Supp. 751 (D.C. Del.)

MT 4231-24   **(12)51**
IR Manual

who is both an attorney and accountant, if they have been made solely to enable him/her to audit the client's books, prepare a federal income tax return, or otherwise act solely as an accountant.[5]

(6) As can be seen by the above court references, the protection accorded privileged communications between client and attorney does not extend to the financial transaction between them. The revenue agent should be able to secure from the attorney any records or information in his/her possession, except those containing the privileged communications, which will aid in his/her audit of the attorney's personal return. This will also be true in situations where the examiner seeks information from an attorney about some other taxpayer. It is well for the revenue agent to realize that a situation concerning privilege could be controversial, and the group manager should be consulted if a problem arises.

(12)52 (8-30-76)   4231
Records

(1) The records that a revenue agent can expect to find in the audit of an attorney's returns will vary. They usually depend on the business arrangement of those involved. In a partnership, or office where there is an associate arrangement, the examiner will usually find complete and adequate records. An attorney's records differ actually in one respect from others, and that is in the maintaining of an account identified as the client's trust fund or escrow account. There may be several accounts, or the attorney may handle all clients' funds through one account.

(2) The records will usually consist of:

    (a) appointment book;

    (b) client's card index;

    (c) a daily log or receipts book;

    (d) a disbursement book or ledger, showing breakdown of regular expenses paid, as well as disbursements made from trust funds;

    (e) individual client's accounts showing description of service, charges and credits;

    (f) case time record per client;

    (g) register of cases in progress, by client's name;

---

[5]Olender v. US., 210 F. 2d 795 (C.A.-9), 54–1 U.S.T.C. 9254; U.S. v. Chin Lim Mow, 12 F.R.D. 433 (N.D., Calif.); in re Fisher, 51 F. 2d 424 (S.D., N.Y.).

    (h) time report per attorney and per client, showing time, dates of work, and billings or charges.

(3) Contrary to a system of complete records maintained in the larger offices, the single attorney, practicing law under less formal office conditions, rarely keeps records in a manner satisfactory to an accountant. However, this does not mean that they are inaccurate or inadequate. They are usually sufficient to record the information that the attorney desires to know. The problem is how to test or audit the available records to determine the accuracy thereof, or to quickly find discrepancies that indicate that the records or manner of recording are inaccurate and necessitate further analysis. The records the examiner may find in this type of office may be:

    (a) an appointment book;

    (b) diary or day book;

    (c) a recording of fees received (many times this is kept by the attorney himself/herself);

    (d) a running account of expenses paid;

    (e) costs relating to a case which may be maintained on the inside page of the folder containing the case file;

    (f) single-entry disbursement book, ledger or sheet;

    (g) monthly recapitulation schedule of fees and expenses;

    (h) duplicate deposit slips, bank statements and cancelled checks.

(12)53 (8-30-76)   4231
Trust Fund or Escrow Account

(1) An accounting feature, peculiar to practicing attorneys, is the trust fund or escrow account. Some States prescribe responsibility for the accounting of client's funds, or funds held in suspense by the attorney. The Canons of Professional Ethics of the American Bar Association, Number 11, dealing with trust property, states: "The lawyer should refrain from any action whereby for his personal benefit or gain he abuses or takes advantage of the confidence reposed in him by his client. Money of the client or collected for the client or other trust property coming into the possession of the lawyer should be reported and accounted for promptly, and should not under any circumstances be commingled with his own or be used by him."

(2) Usually the attorney will deposit into this account funds received from the client which will be subject to disbursement for various reasons. Some will apply to the attorney's fee, some will be disbursed to other attorneys, other parties to a suit, other parties to a transaction, and expenses. Good practice dictates that the attorney clearly withdraw funds for his/her fee, and record it in another part of his/her records, but this is not always done. The revenue agent must be alert and carefully analyze disbursements from the fund, and make an accurate accounting of the identity of the funds making up the balance of the account at the end of the period. It has been found that some attorneys misuse the trust fund account to the extent of holding portions of funds in the trust fund account which are actually earned fees or unexpended cost advances. This is difficult to detect, since it could well be that the attorney would be in a position to take alternative actions, or exercise options. Substantial amounts held for any length of time should be investigated to the extent that the examiner is satisfied that the fee income is reported, and in the proper year.

(3) By tracing the payment of funds to other attorneys out of the trust account, the examiner can verify the correctness of the disbursement and also verify that the payment was reported by the recipient.

(4) It is well to remember that attorneys' activities might encompass the whole field of business. He/she may be a specialist in any number of fields (corporation attorney, estates and trusts, criminal, general trial, income tax, grower associations). He/she may be an expert in real estate, giving legal advice in these transactions, and perhaps in some instances be a party to the transaction itself. If the attorney is engaged in investments or speculative transactions, as well as in a professional capacity, the revenue agent should probe the situation to be certain that the true tax liability for all parties concerned is accurately reported.

(5) The revenue agent should be alert to determine that the attorney has disclosed all special accounts, all accounts with associates, all trust fund accounts (since there may be more than one), and all partnership accounts.

(12)54 (8-30-76)   4231
Source of Fees

(1) A practicing attorney's principal source of income is from fees received for representing clients in any number of situations. Some sources of fees are from divorce actions, civil actions, trial work, probate work, estates, taxes, legal representation in negotiations for sale or purchase, referral from other attorneys, operation of collection agency or collector of accounts, fees from banks for servicing wills or other service, patents, admiralty law, and lobbyists' fees.

(2) Determining the value of promotional stock or other assets received by an attorney in lieu of a fee for services has always been a problem. The examiner should be aware that attorneys may receive such assets at the time of organizing a new corporation or negotiating a favorable situation.

(3) Sometimes an attorney will attempt to convey the impression that securities, bonds, or other assets, were received as gifts. It has been arranged, in some instances, that the attorney will be the residual beneficiary of an estate. The examiner should ask the taxpayer if any property has been or will be received. If the answer is in the affirmative, the examination should be pursued so that the true facts can be interpreted.

(4) In criminal cases fees are usually demanded in advance. In most cases, attorneys consider this to be the total fee. This is so, especially if the case is lost. Many attorneys maintain a folder for each case, not necessarily by client, so that one person could have several folders. This is well to remember when determining all fees paid by a particular client.

(5) In many areas, members of bar associations have established minimum fee schedules. The use of such a schedule, if available, would assist the examiner in testing the recorded fee income. Any income found by the agent to be inconsistent with the schedule will provide him/her with a good opportunity to discuss the reason for the variance with the attorney. Such a discussion may develop unreported cases and test the accuracy of the records.

(6) Types of fee arrangement include single retainer fees, annual retainer fees, contingent fees, and referral fees. The single retainer fee may be received in advance, in full or in part. The annual retainer fee may be received monthly or at other intervals. Contingent fees are based upon a percentage of amounts collected or recovered. Referral fees are received from other attorneys to whom clients are referred for services.

(7) In cases with inadequate records the following sources of information may be helpful in securing leads to names of clients an attorney may be representing. It would be necessary to

contact the client to determine the amount of fee paid. Local court dockets and legal newspapers contain names of attorneys representing clients before local courts. Certain administrative agencies, such as the Workmen's Compensation Commission, often maintain lists of the names of attorneys who have represented clients before their agencies. In insurance claim cases, regional index bureaus have information on attorneys which may be helpful. Any casualty insurance company can supply the name and address of the index bureau for the State of the taxpayer under examination. The amount of the information available will depend on the recordkeeping system of each index bureau.

(8) The examiner may occassionally find an attorney reporting a fee claimed to be earned over a 36-month period or more and coming under section 1301, as originally enacted. These original relief provisions apply to taxable years beginning before 1964 or, if elected by the taxpayer, to years beginning after 1963 provided "employment" began before February 6, 1963.

(9) With the exception of this election, for taxable years beginning after 1963, the income averaging provisions of IRC 1301-1305 would apply.

(10) In the event either situation exists, the examiner should determine whether the relief provisions are applicable.

(11) Practicing attorneys may also receive income from teaching and writing.

(12)55 (8-30-76)   4231
Expenses

(1) Many expenses of attorneys, such as rent and utilities, are similar to those of other professional persons. In addition to these similar expenses, an attorney often has expenses in behalf of a client.

(2) If the attorney's right to reimbursement is not contingent upon any event, though the timing of the reimbursement may be, then, as a general rule, the amounts expended on behalf of clients are not deductible in the year expended.

(3) If reimbursement is contingent upon successful completion of the case—a usual practice in personal injury actions—the amounts expended by the attorney would be deductible in the year expended provided they meet IRC 162's requirement of ordinary and necessary.

(4) If the amounts expended are for personal living expenses of the client and reimbursement is contingent upon successful completion

of the case, there is authority for holding that the expenditures do not meet the requirements of ordinary and necessary under IRC 162 (W. Burnett, 356 F. 2d 755).

(5) The examiner should determine the proper treatment of expenses, advances and reimbursements in this area which will invariably require an analysis of the attorney's trust account.

(6) The examiner should satisfy himself/herself that any contributions to election campaigns of state, county and local officials have not been claimed as business expenses.

(12)60 (8-30-76)   4231
Engineers

(1) Engineers are usually subject to registration in the various States in order to operate on a professional basis. The work of the engineer is divided into several highly specialized fields and includes designing, estimating, supervising construction, and consulting, among other related activities. The major fields of specialization are civil, chemical, electrical, and mechanical engineering.

(2) Civil engineers make land surveys and maps, and generally plan and supervise heavy construction, such as buildings, roads, and bridges. Chemical engineers are called upon in the planning and operation of chemical plants.

(3) Electrical engineers are specialists in the electrical and electronic fields. Mechanical engineers design and supervise installation and operation of heavy machinery and heating plants.

(4) The income of professional engineers consists of fees which are usually received according to the terms of a contract. A written contract should exist between the engineer and his/her principal for each job undertaken. The contract should include a description of the services to be rendered, an estimate of the time required to perform the work, and the terms for the settlement of the fee.

(5) Fees may be received upon the completion of work or when it is delivered and accepted, or progressively as the work is completed. It is not unusual to find that the engineering services on long-term contracts are paid for according to the percentage of completion of the job, or in installments over the period of the project.

(6) Engineering firms may report income by the cash receipts and disbursements method, or by the accrual method, where they are engaged in an engineering capacity and are not functioning as the general contractors. In the latter case, the methods of accounting available to contractors would be available.

(7) Generally, the larger engineering firms report income by the accrual method. The accruals are usually computed by the percentage of completion method on long-term contracts or by the completed contract method.

(8) The examination of the accounts of an engineering firm presents no unusual problems. The contracts should be available for the verification of income, and the specific job costs can usually be related directly to the income items. Estimates of the percentage of completion of the jobs in progress at the end of the period are usually available for the verification of reportable income. In addition to the verification of income, there is one item which should be particularly investigated in the examination of an engineering firm. A reconciliation should be made of the amounts paid to engineer employees with the amounts reported on W-2 forms.

(12)70 (8–30–76)   4231
Architects

(1) The profession of the architect is in some respects similar to that of the engineer. The architect is employed to design buildings and to supervise their construction to see that it conforms to specifications. His/her income is derived from fees.

(2) The compensation of the architect is sometimes a fixed percentage of costs of construction. It is also based on direct labor costs plus an allowance for overhead, fees for consultants, etc. The compensation is usually paid in installments, the first payment being made when the contract is signed. Other installments may be received as the work progresses, with full settlement when the completed structure is accepted.

(3) There are occasions when the architect is issued stocks or securities in the corporation for which he/she has performed services. The examining agent should be aware of the possibility that this type of transaction has been negotiated.

(4) When contractors bid on the construction designed by the architect, they are usually required to deposit performance guarantees with the architect as security for the building plans and specifications used in making their estimates. The deposits are returnable to the contractor when the performance is completed. Until such time, the architect reports the deposit as a liability. The return of the deposit is not an expense.

(5) The architect may be called upon to make advances on behalf of his/her client, such as for the purchase of certain equipment which the client is obligated to furnish. This type of transaction is an account receivable until satisfied. It should not be charged as an expense.

(6) A large item of expenditure by architects is for blueprints and supplies. The costs of blueprints are usually charged to the cost of specific jobs.

(7) Usually contracts are signed with clients for the specific jobs, wherein the basis of compensation is defined. The examining agent should examine these contracts in connection with the verification of the fees recorded.

(8) Sources of information on the activity of architects include building permits issued, newspaper items on construction, and the examination of third parties.

(9) The accounts peculiar to architects are: Advances for clients, fees to engineers and consultants, and blueprints. These items are usually charged to the specific costs of jobs for which the expenditures were made or to accounts receivable.

(10) Income may be reported by the cash receipts and disbursements method or by the accrual method, in cases where the architect's income is purely from fees. Where the architect is also engaged in contracting, the methods available to contractors are available to him/her, i.e., the percentage of completion method, or the completed contract method.

(11) The examination of the return of an architect does not generally present any features not found in other types of business. The agent should be alert to any indication that reported income does not include all fees received. The examination of the expenses deducted follows the general procedures of other types of examination.

(12)80 (8–30–76)   4231
Funeral Directors

(1) In examining the income of funeral directors, public records are available in determining whether income from all funerals have been reported. Death certificates, executed by physicians or coroners, are filed with a Bureau of Vital Statistics or Public Health Department. Also permits for removal or burial of the bodies of deceased persons must be issued by public officials upon each death. Obituary news in local papers may state the name of the undertaker.

(2) The charges made by the undertaking establishment to the account of a funeral are for the following items:
    (a) sale of caskets and vaults;
    (b) sale of clothing;

(c) compensation for services rendered;

(d) reimbursement for cash outlay.

(3) One basis of charges is for specific items of service rendered, such as the price of the casket, the use of the chapel, limousines, casket bearers, etc. But a more prevalent basis of charges now in use is the setting of an all-inclusive price covering every essential detail, based on the cost of the selected casket plus other articles supplied and the value of various services rendered. The style of the casket is used as the basis for unit prices charged. The style and cost of a casket can be used as an indication of the amount being charged for the funeral services. The profit on the casket is the chief source of income, even though billing is usually made as a flat price for the complete service. Income may be received from the sale of the deceased person's clothing.

(4) Cash outlays are made for certain items, and are charged to the account receivable for reimbursement. Items such as newspaper advertising, cemetery fees, burial clothing, hiring of pallbearers, rental of vehicles, transportation of decedent by air or rail, and honorariums to ministers represent typical items for which cash outlays are made.

(5) Often the undertaking establishment is paid by the survivors of the deceased by tendering an insurance check for the proceeds of a life insurance policy. This may be in excess of the total funeral charges, and the excess is refunded to the beneficiary of the policy by the issue of a check by the undertaker. A test of the refunds should be made by the agent to verify that such check issued is not entered as a deduction. There have been instances where this has occurred. A reconciliation of cash receipts with bank deposits and with income recorded may reveal that cash receipts include the insurance checks, but the recorded income is not in balance with the receipts by the amount of the excess of the insurance checks over the funeral charges. Yet the refunds may be deducted as an expense item. This method results in an unallowable deduction of the amount refunded.

(6) The inventories of a funeral director include caskets, casket materials and supplies, embalming supplies, and miscellaneous supplies. The most significant item in the inventory is the caskets.

(7) In examining the returns of a funeral director, the revenue agent should be aware that there may be death certificates filed without

corresponding burial permits, and vice versa. This comes about through deaths of visitors or of residents who are buried in other places than the city of the funeral director. Where items such as advertising, cemetery fees, pallbearers, etc., are being deducted as expenses of the undertaking establishment instead of being charged to accounts receivable, the examiner should make sufficient inquiry to determine that reimbursement was not made to the undertaker for those items in addition to the charges for services. Normally, such items are charged to accounts receivable and not to expense.

(8) Arranging for funeral services prior to death and the payment of so-called preneed funds to the funeral director is a growing practice. The examiner should determine that the funds received as well as income earned on the funds are properly handled for tax purposes.

(12)90 (8-30-76)   4231
Real Estate Brokers

(1) Real estate brokers engage in the management of properties for landlords and in the sales of real estate for owners. A percentage of the rents received or of the selling price of the property is received by the broker for his/her services. An agency relationship exists between the broker and his/her principal.

(2) Examiners should be aware that brokers often receive property other than money for their services, such as second deeds of trust. A determination should be made that such receipt is properly accounted for as well as any interest received on the other property.

(3) A real estate agency often is licensed by one or more insurance companies to write fire, automobile, and casualty insurance.

(4) Some real estate brokers, in addition to the above activities, buy real estate for resale on their own account or for investment purposes. Under these circumstances the examiner will often have to determine whether the real estate sold was purchased by the broker for resale, or whether it was originally purchased for investment. Where the sale is claimed as a capital transaction, the agent should require the submission of proof by the taxpayer that the property was not purchased primarily for resale. Very often the properties are purchased to be held until a satisfactory sale can be effected. In the meantime, the property is rented to a tenant and depreciation is claimed. It should be borne in mind that the deduction of depreciation is not determinative of intent.

(5) The agent should be alert to situations which would in fact be rentals with options to purchase. Examination of contracts will usually reveal the true intent of the parties. An examination of the broker's copies of sales agreements and settlement sheets will assist in determining when sales were consummated, thus indicating when commissions should be included in income.

(6) Sources of information on real estate dealer's transactions are records of deed transfers, mortgages, title company records, banks, mortgage companies, and savings and loan associations. Where a broker deals on his/her own account the financial establishments usually have statements of his/her net worth in their files. These statements may be useful in verifying that the broker's activities are properly reflected in his/her records.

(7) Where the broker also sells insurance, additional accounts will appear in his/her records reflecting accounts receivable from policy holders and accounts payable to insurance companies.

(8) The insurance companies require their agents to render monthly "Accounts Current" reflecting the issue and the cancellation of policies. The premium charged, commissions earned, cash received, and balance due are recorded for each policy issued. A carbon copy of the "Account Current" is retained by the broker, and is often referred to as the policy register. This register provides a means of verifying the insurance transactions. There should be a monthly policy register for each insurance company represented.

(9) Also see Techniques Handbook for Specialized Industries—Construction and Real Estate, IRM 4232.7.

Index